My Fir

Christmas

Advent Calendar

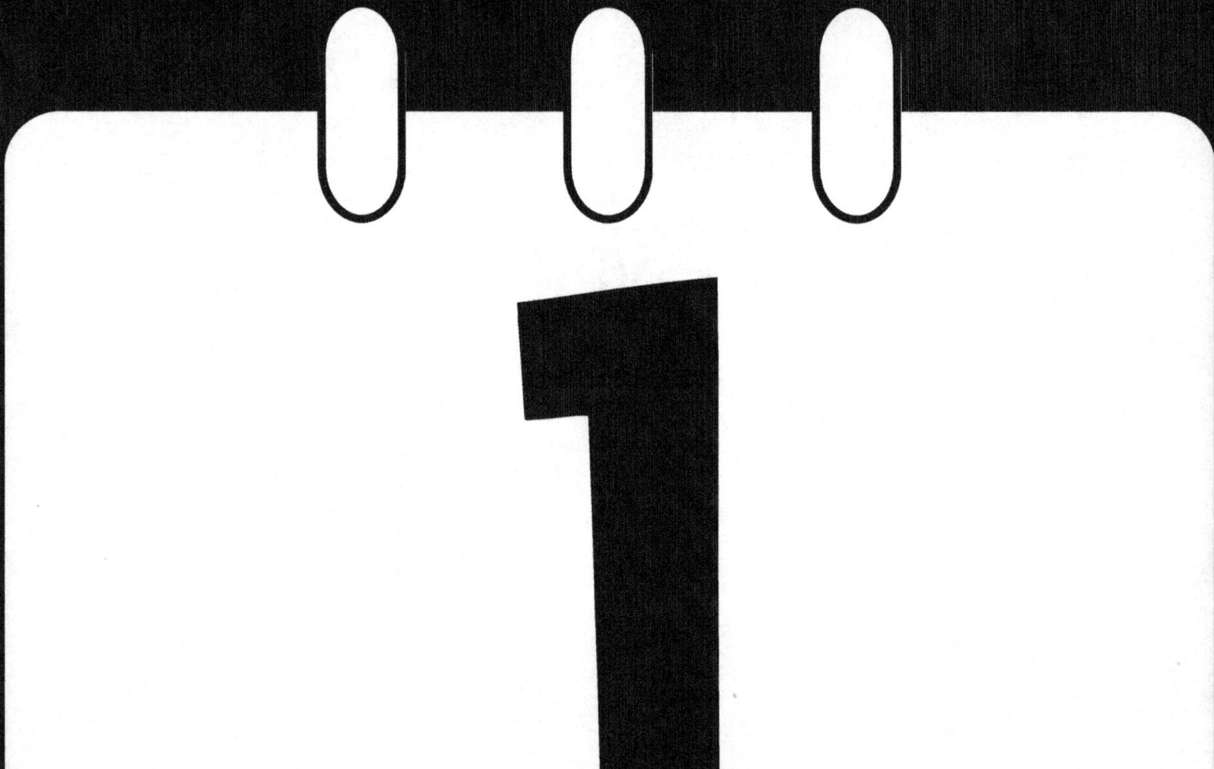
1

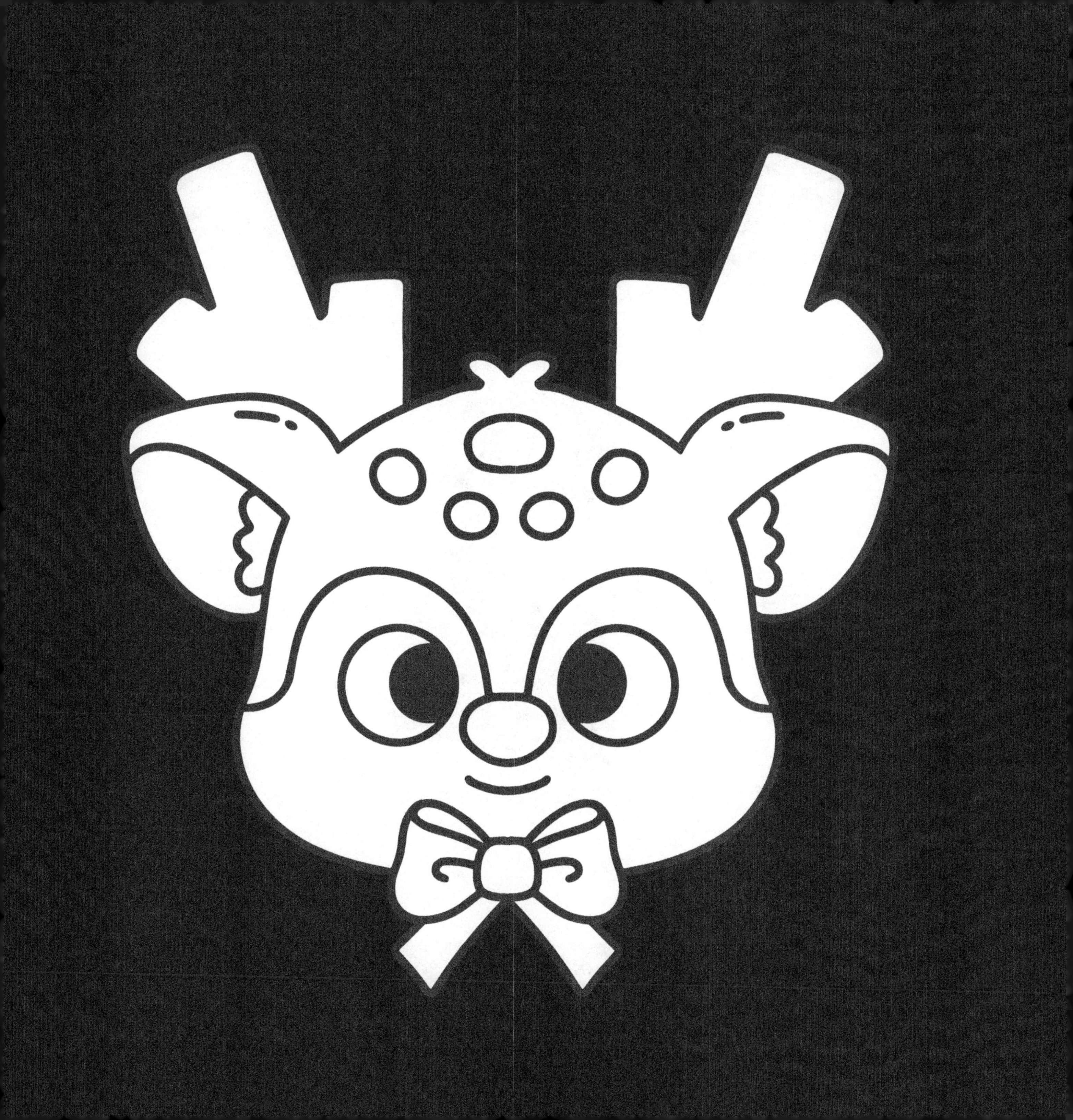

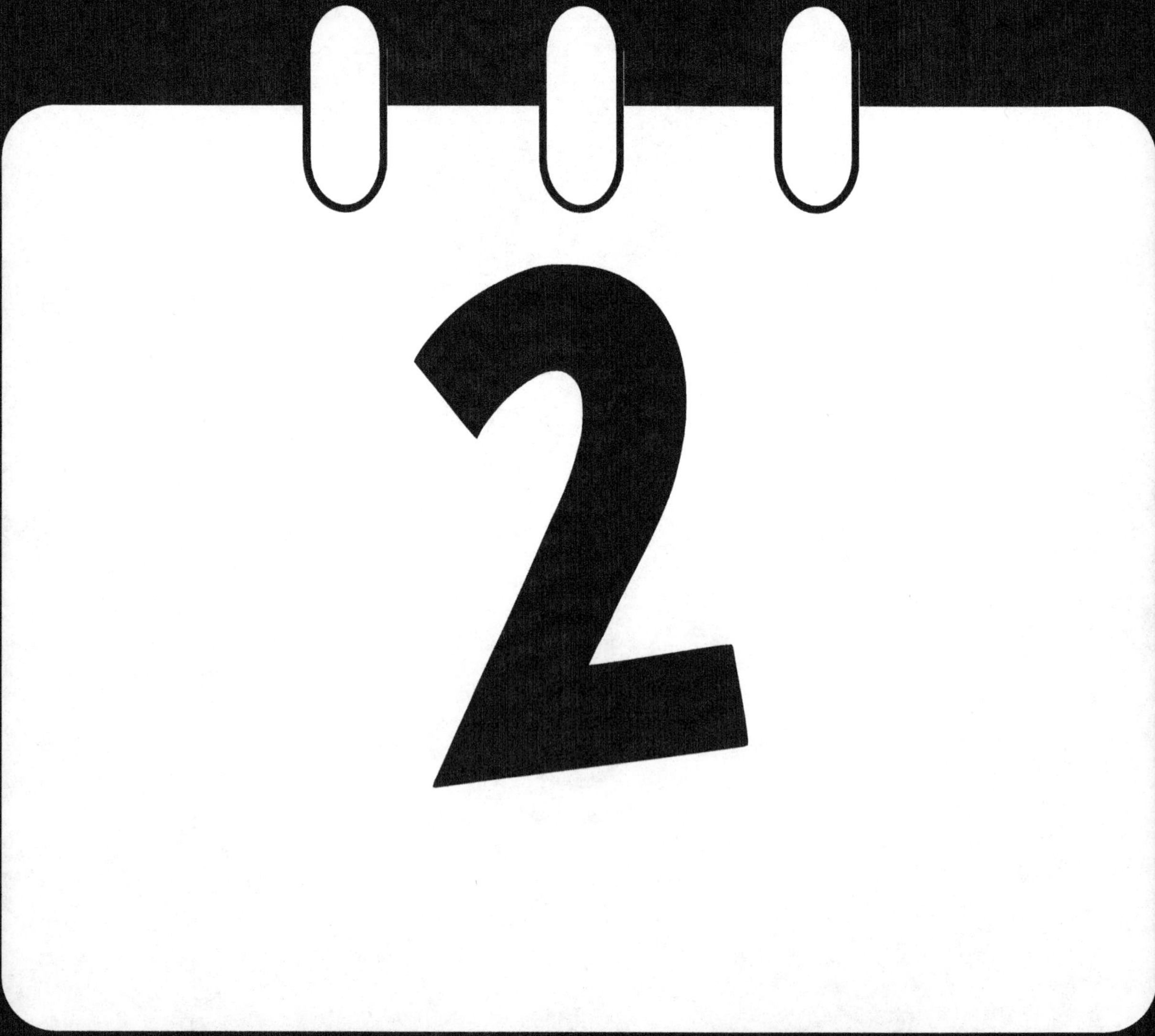
2

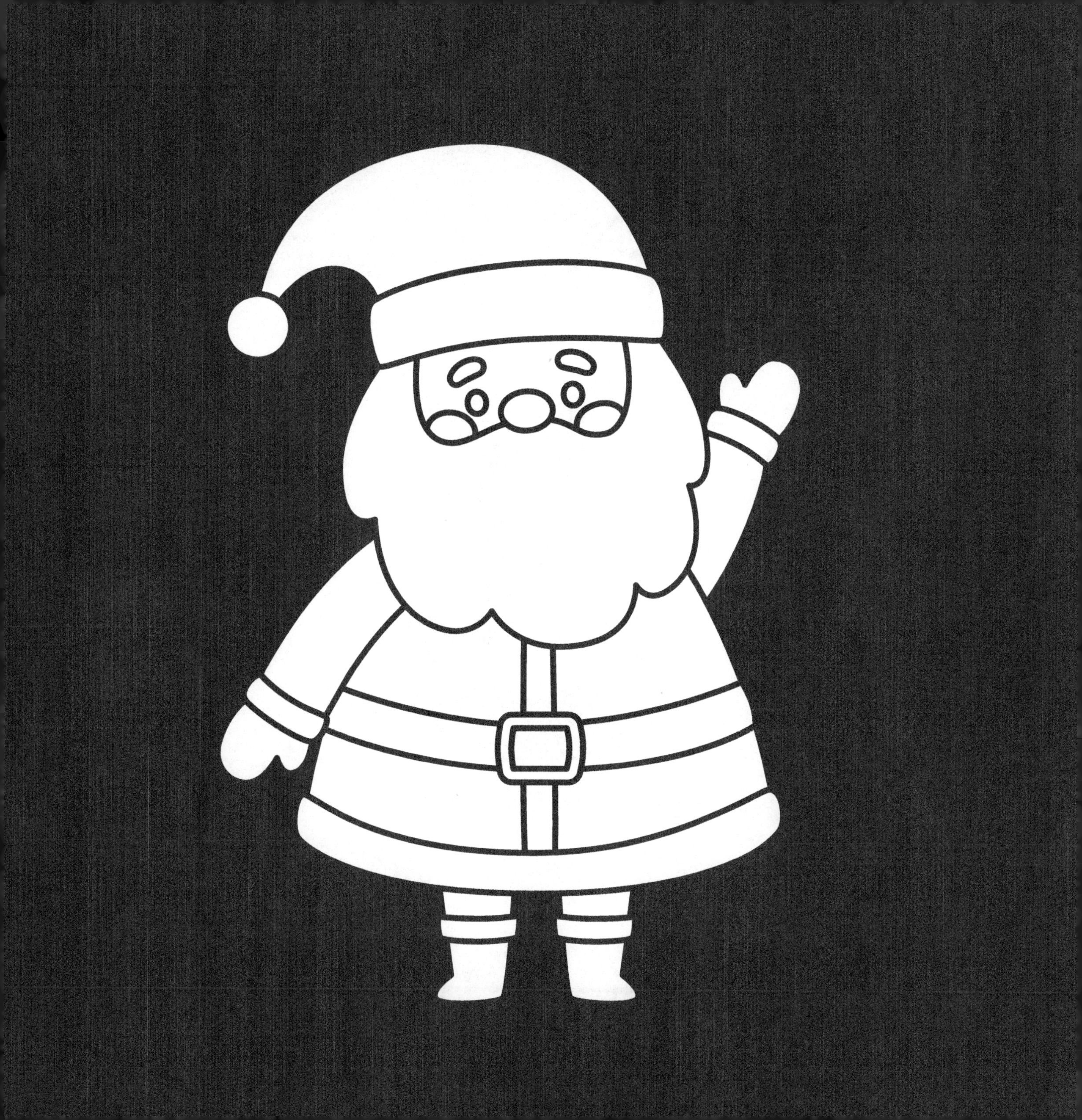

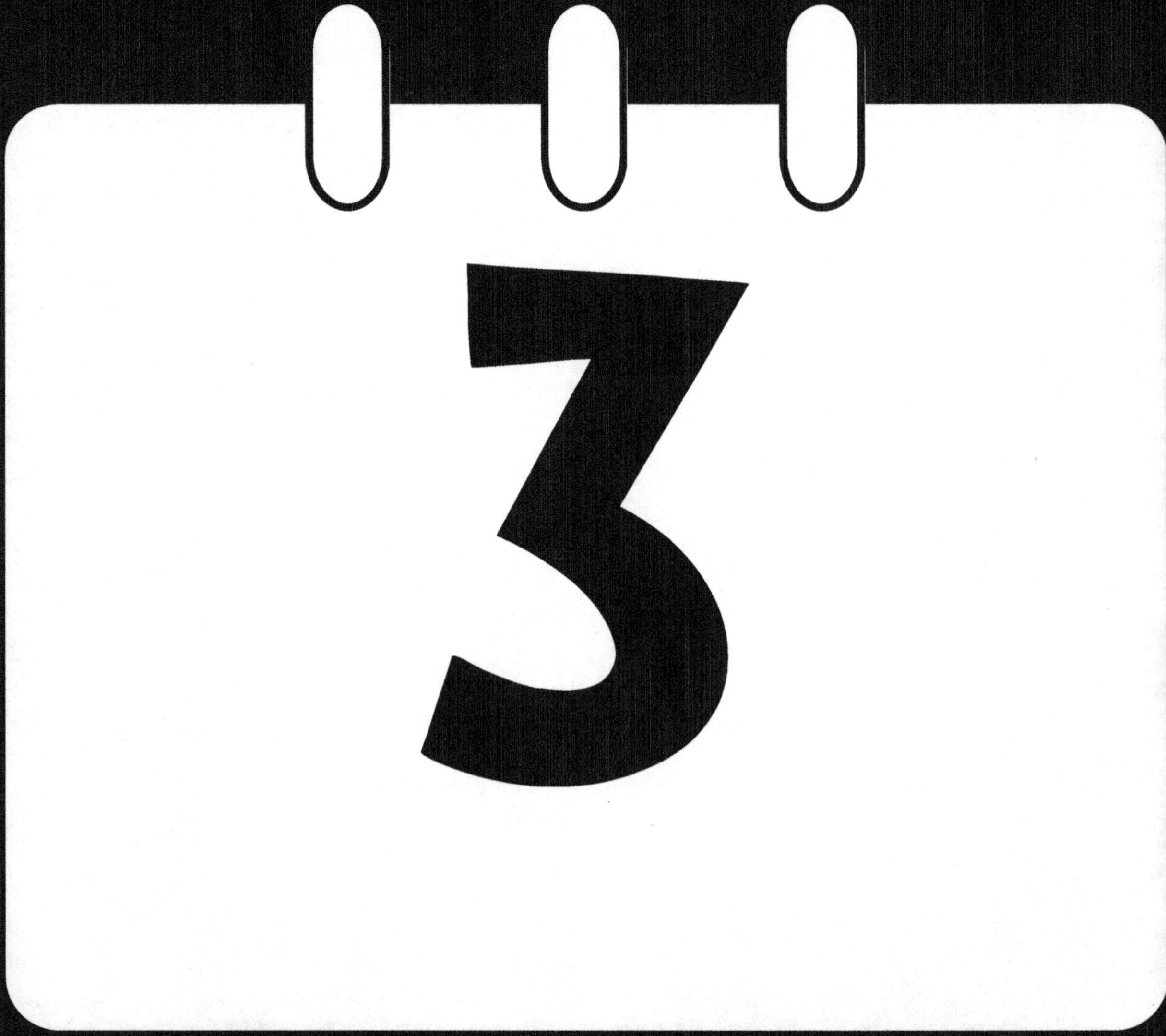
3

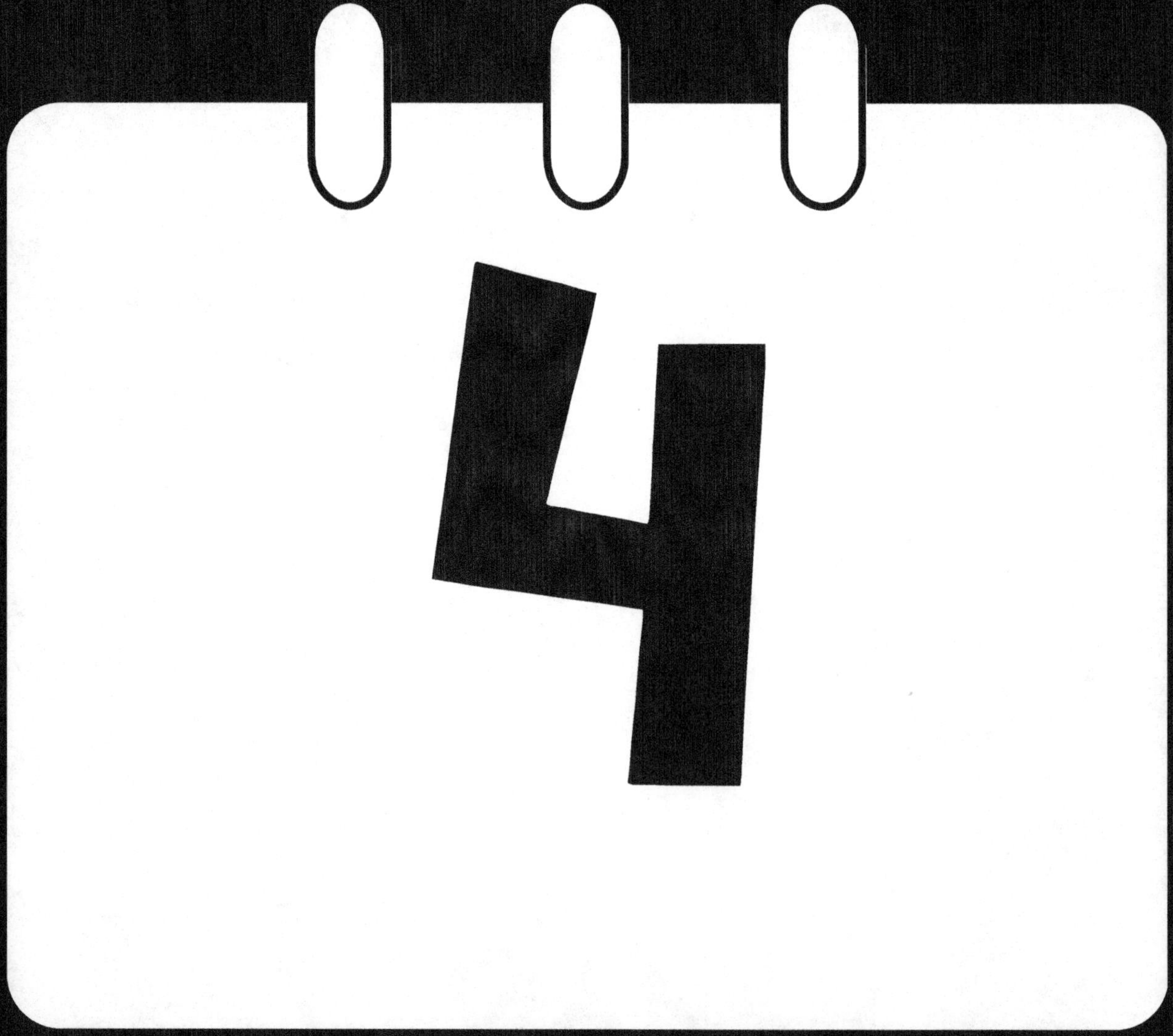
4

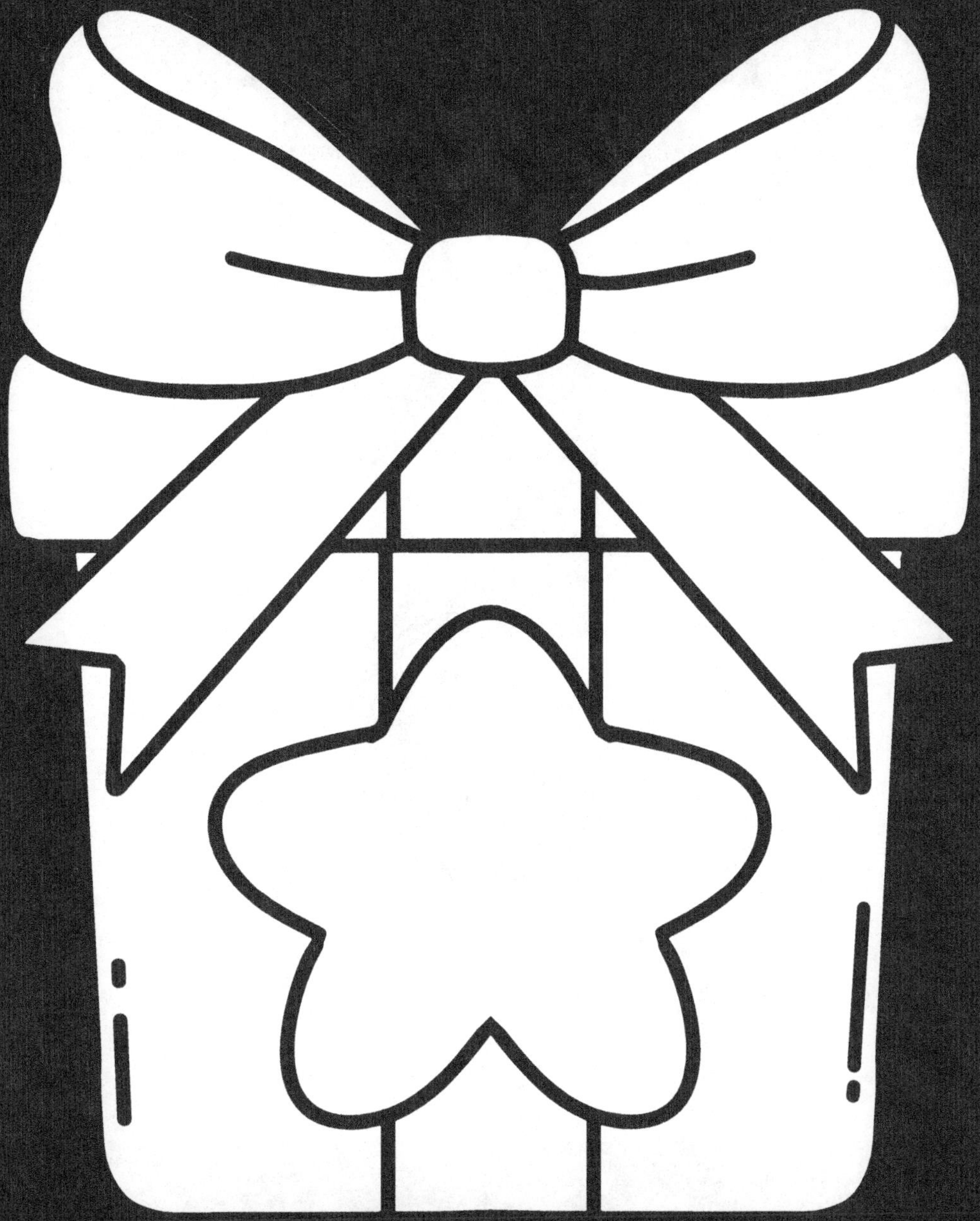

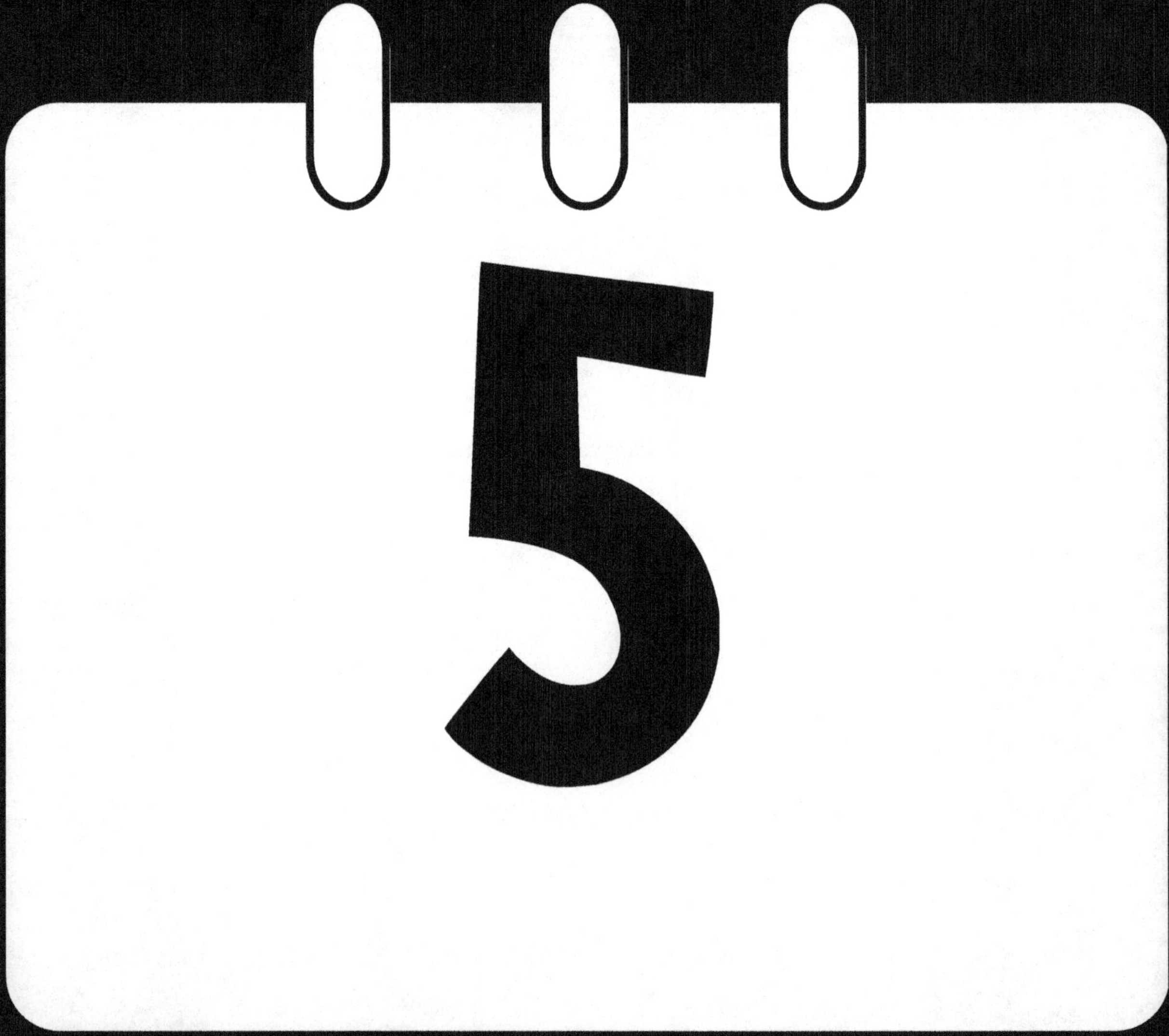
5

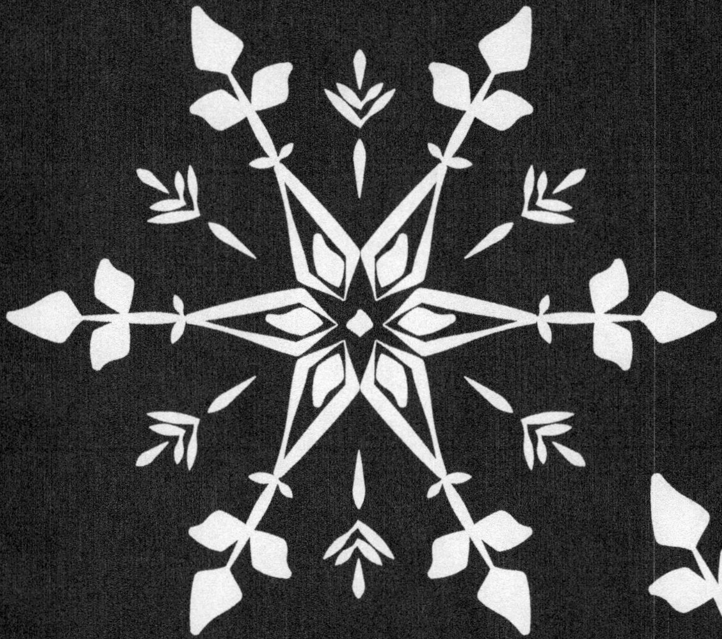
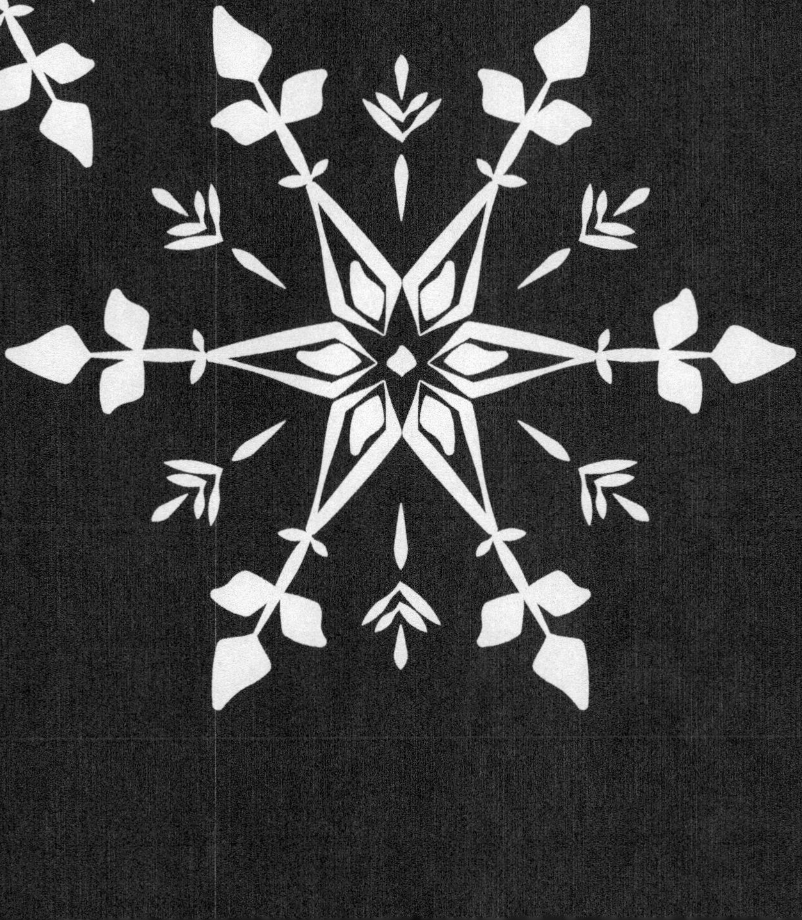

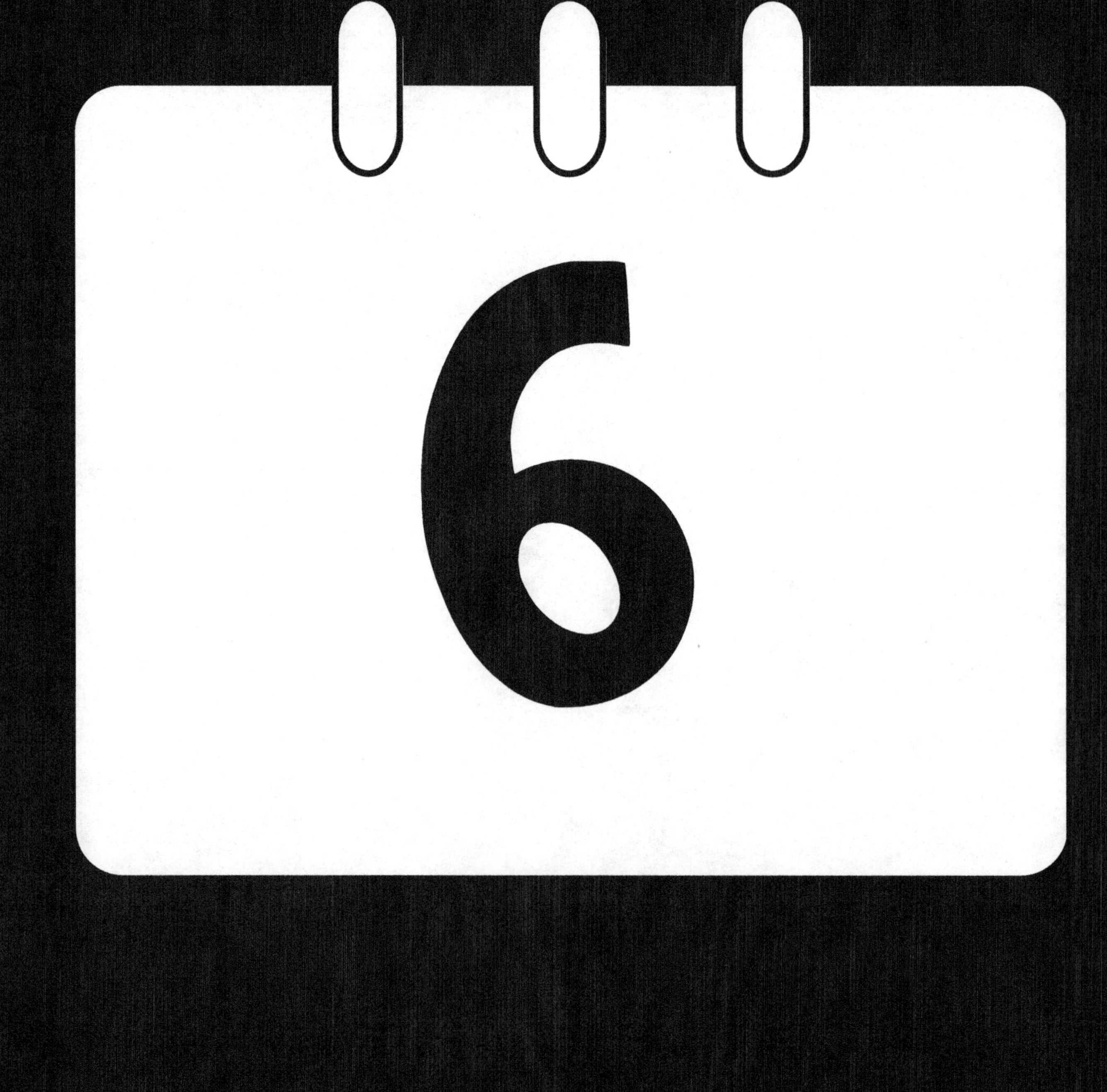
6

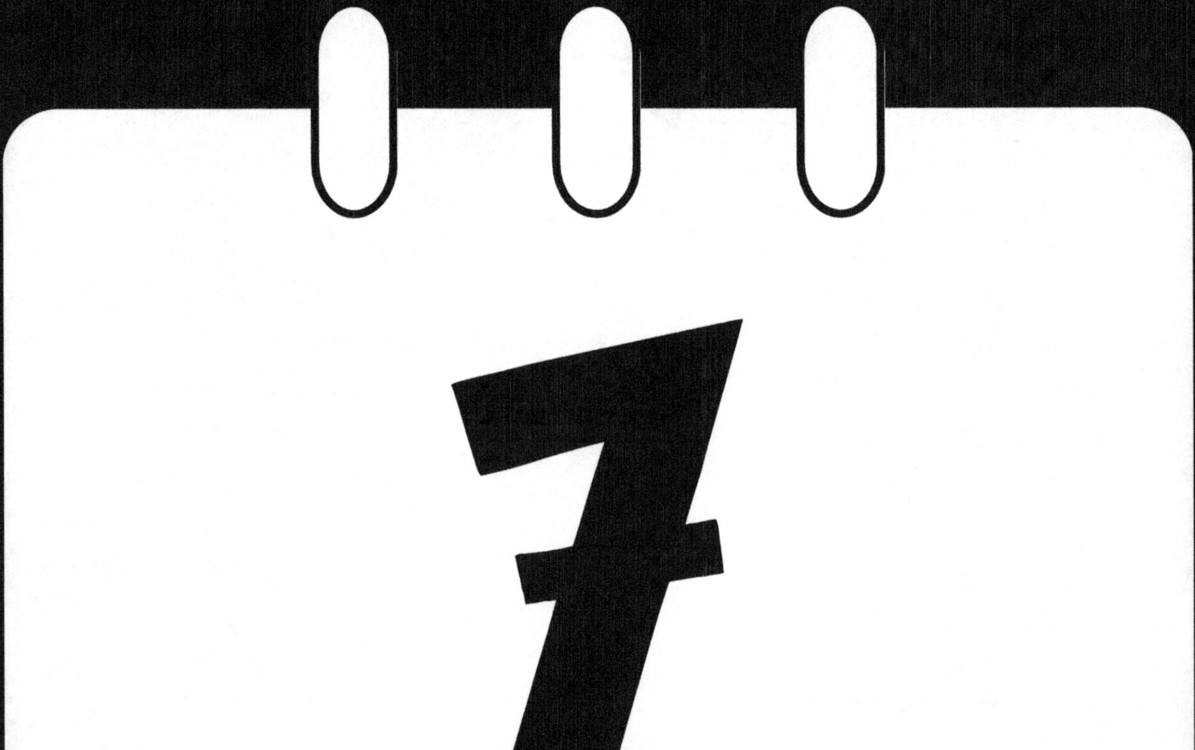
7

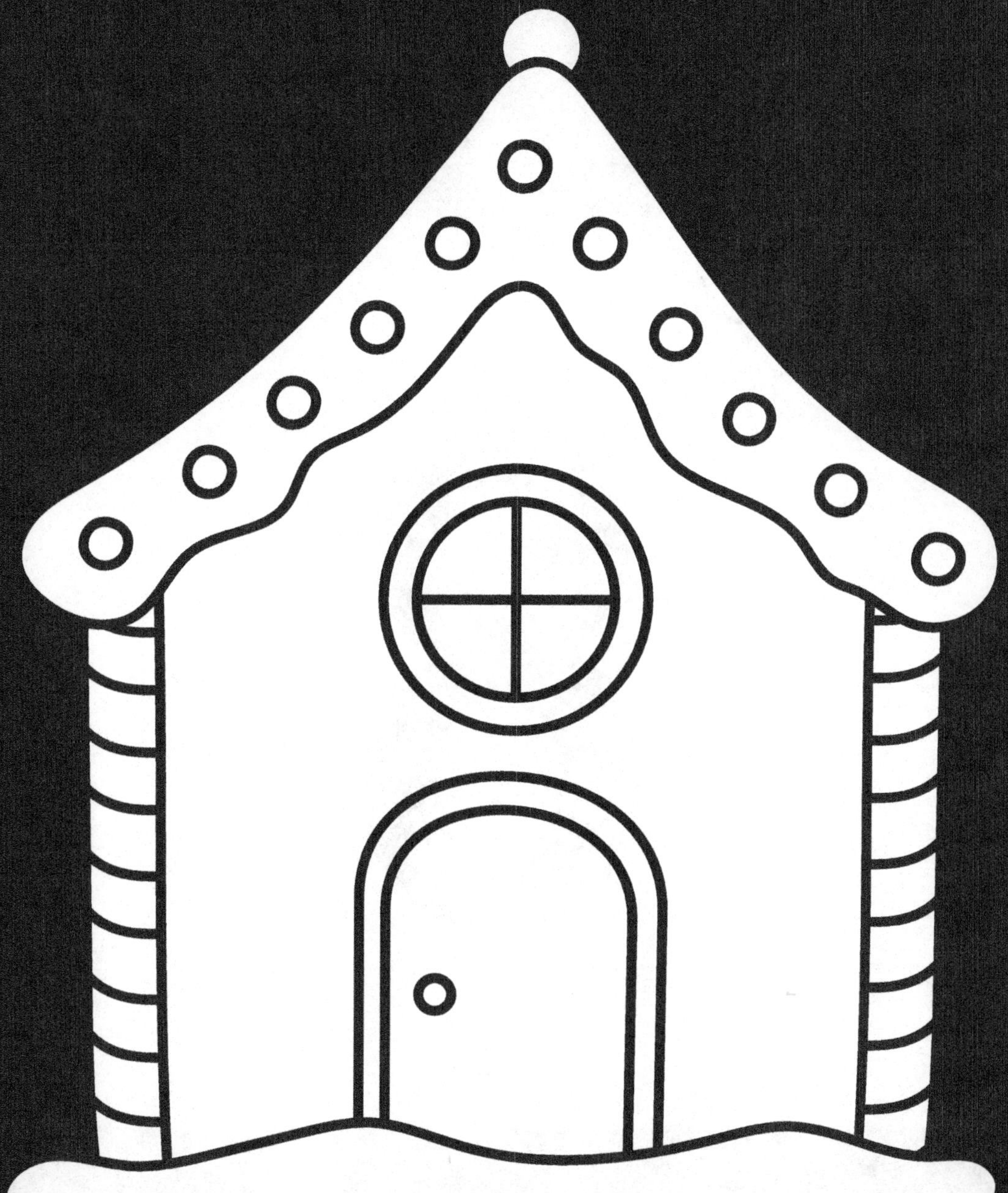

8

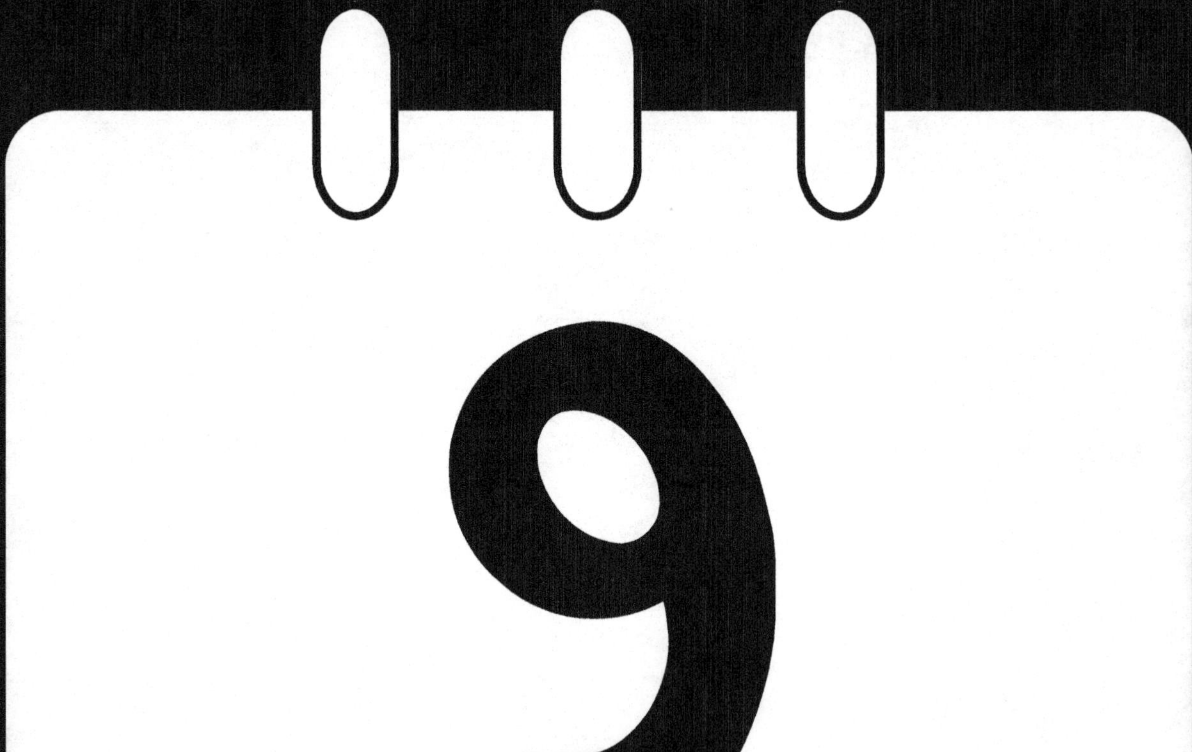
9

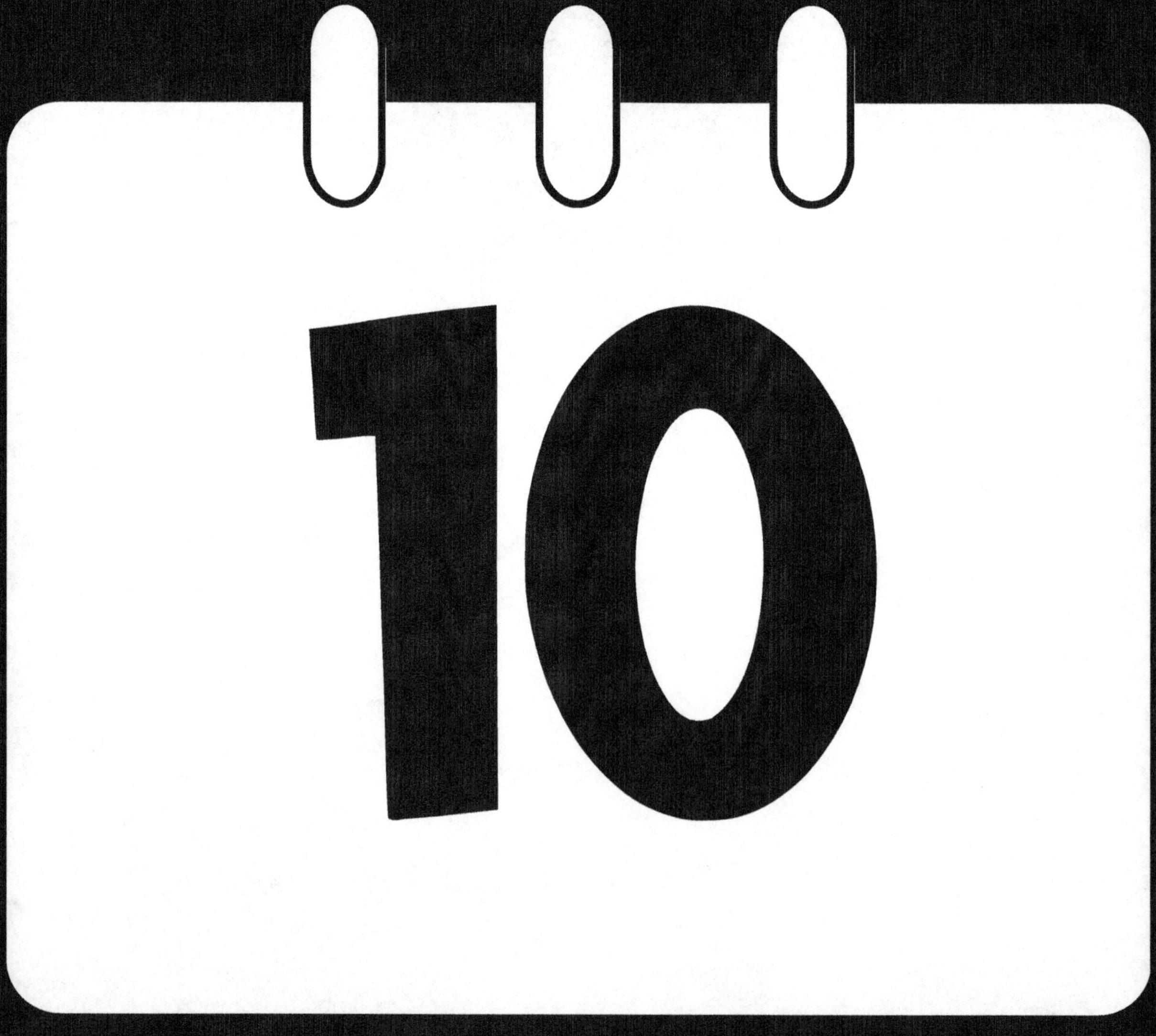
10

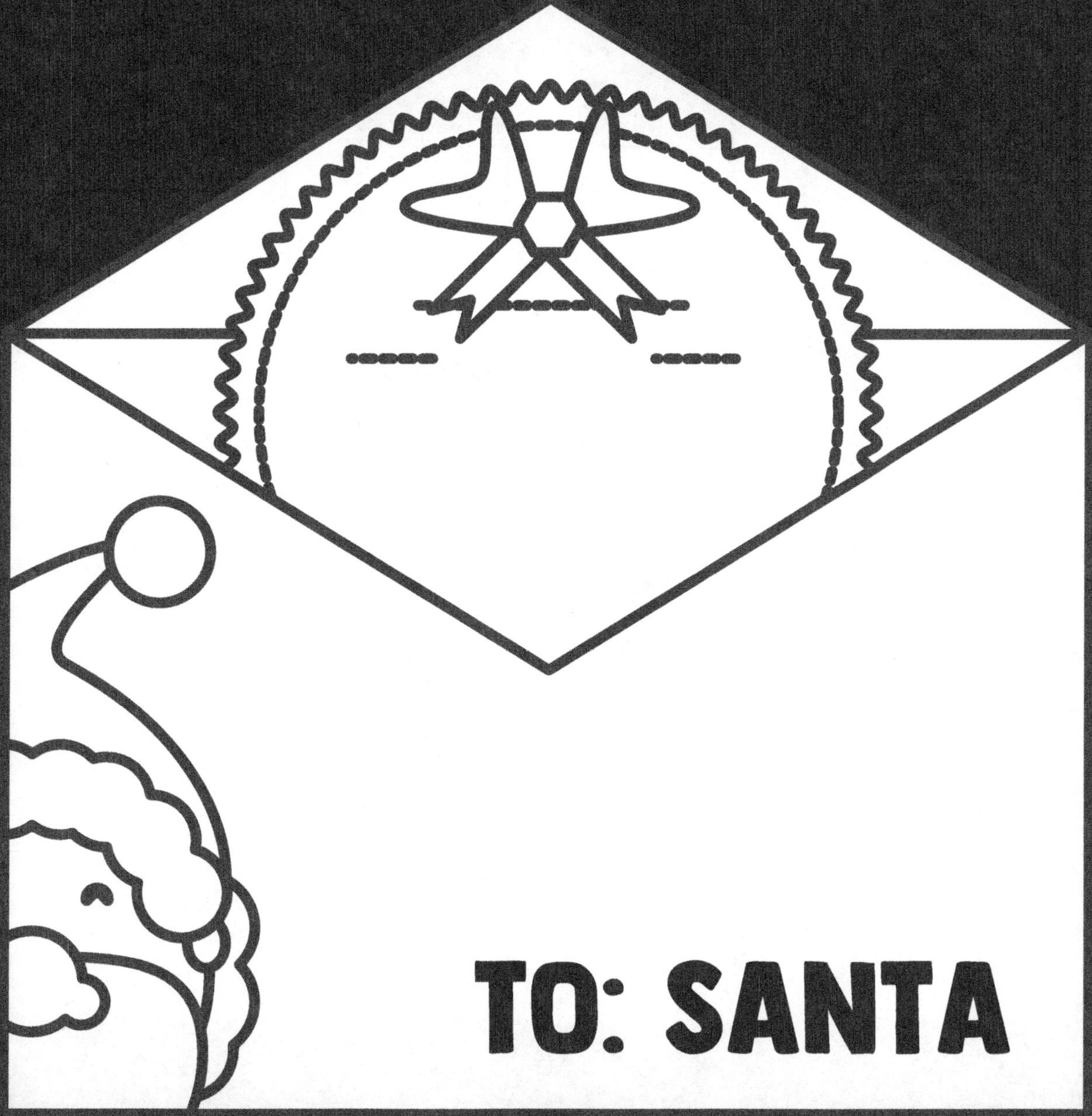
TO: SANTA

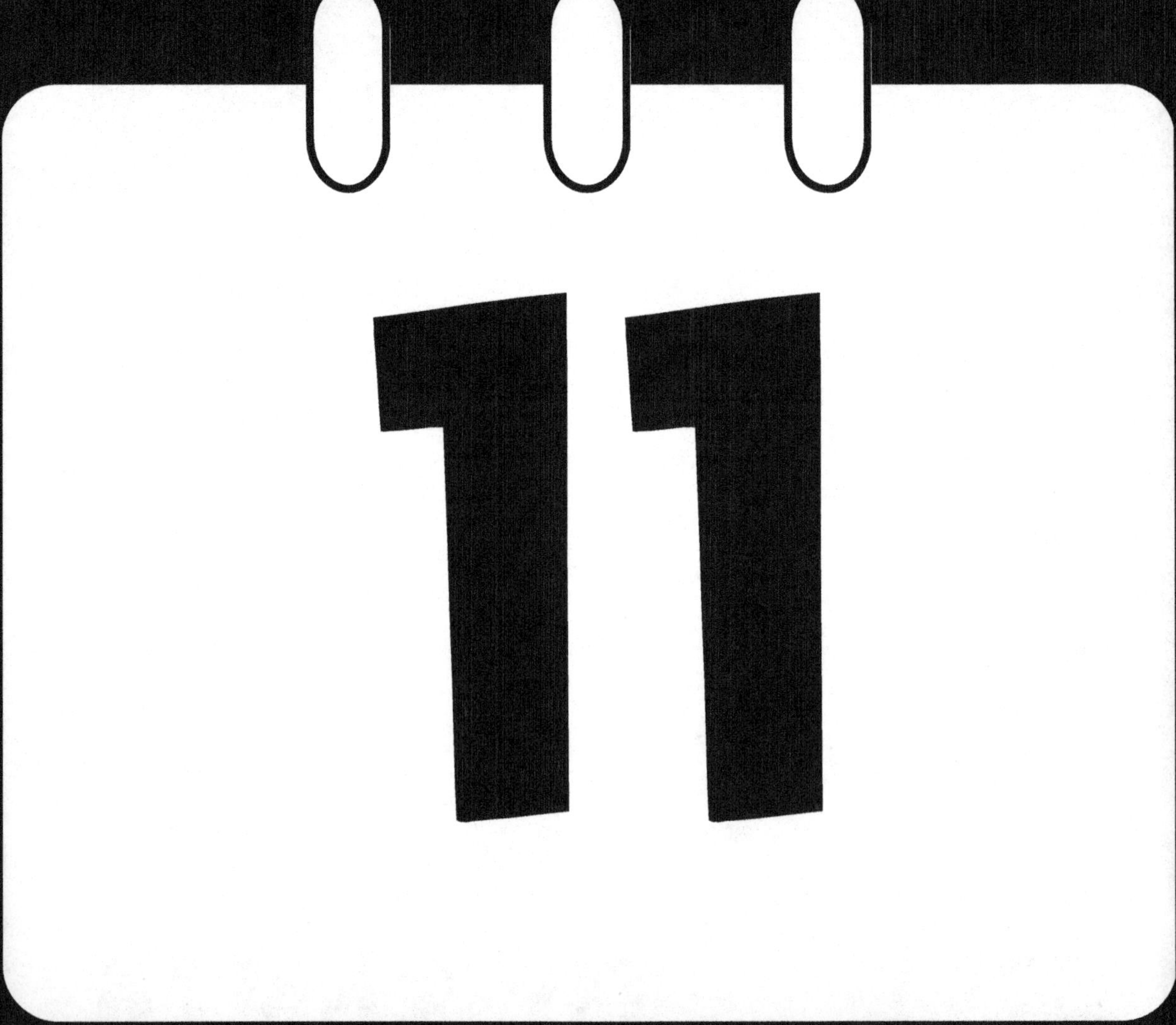
11

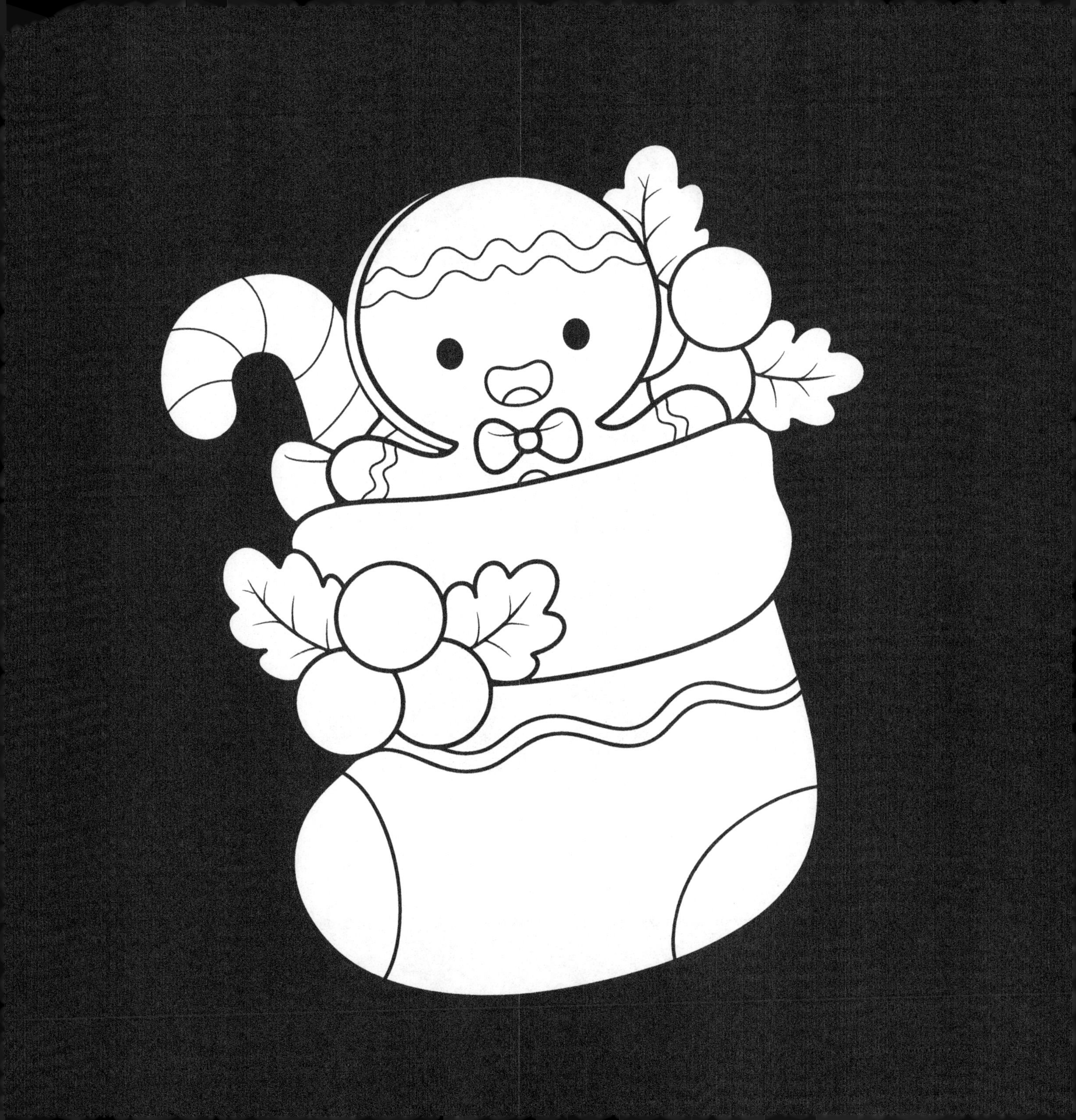

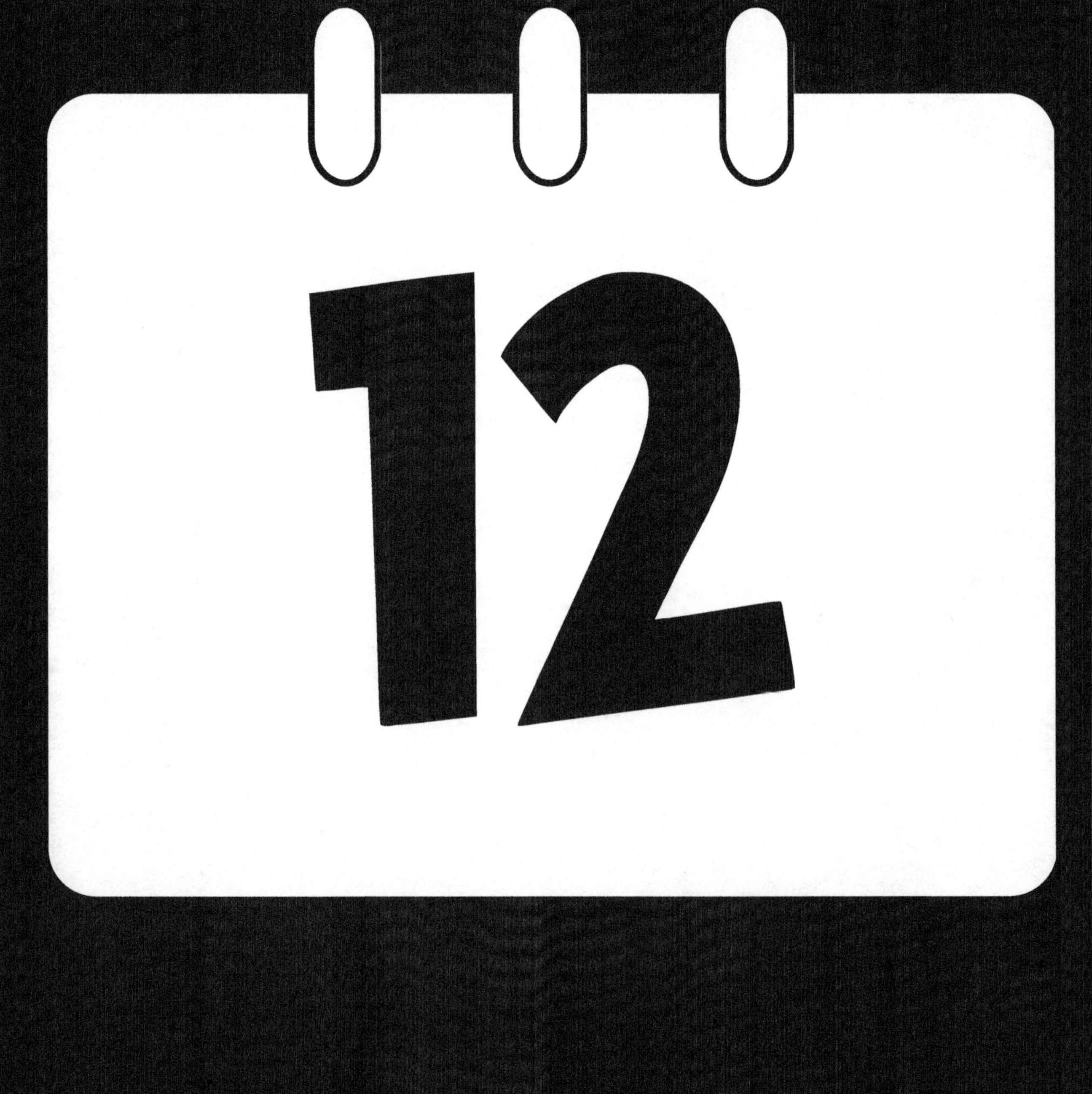
12

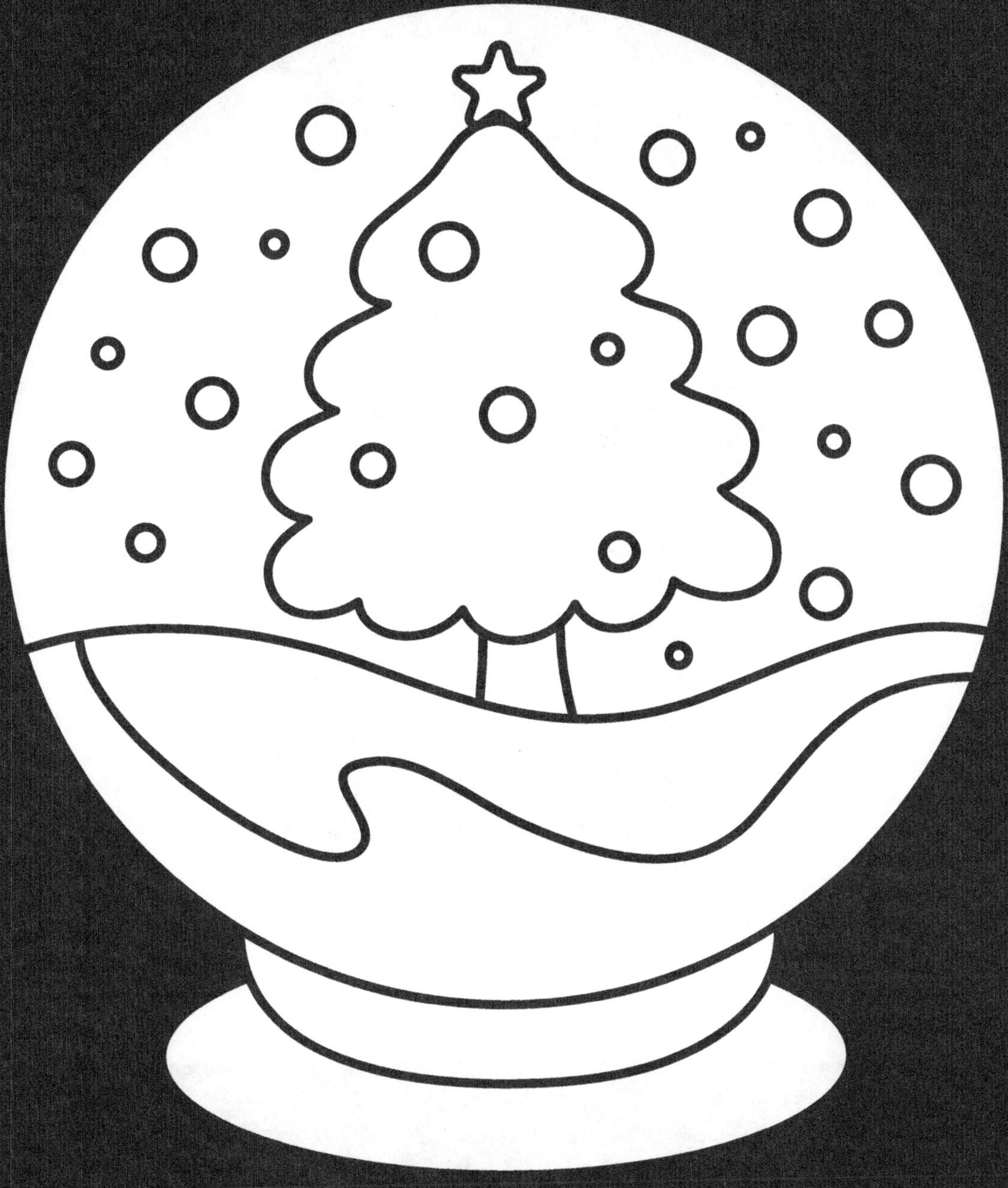

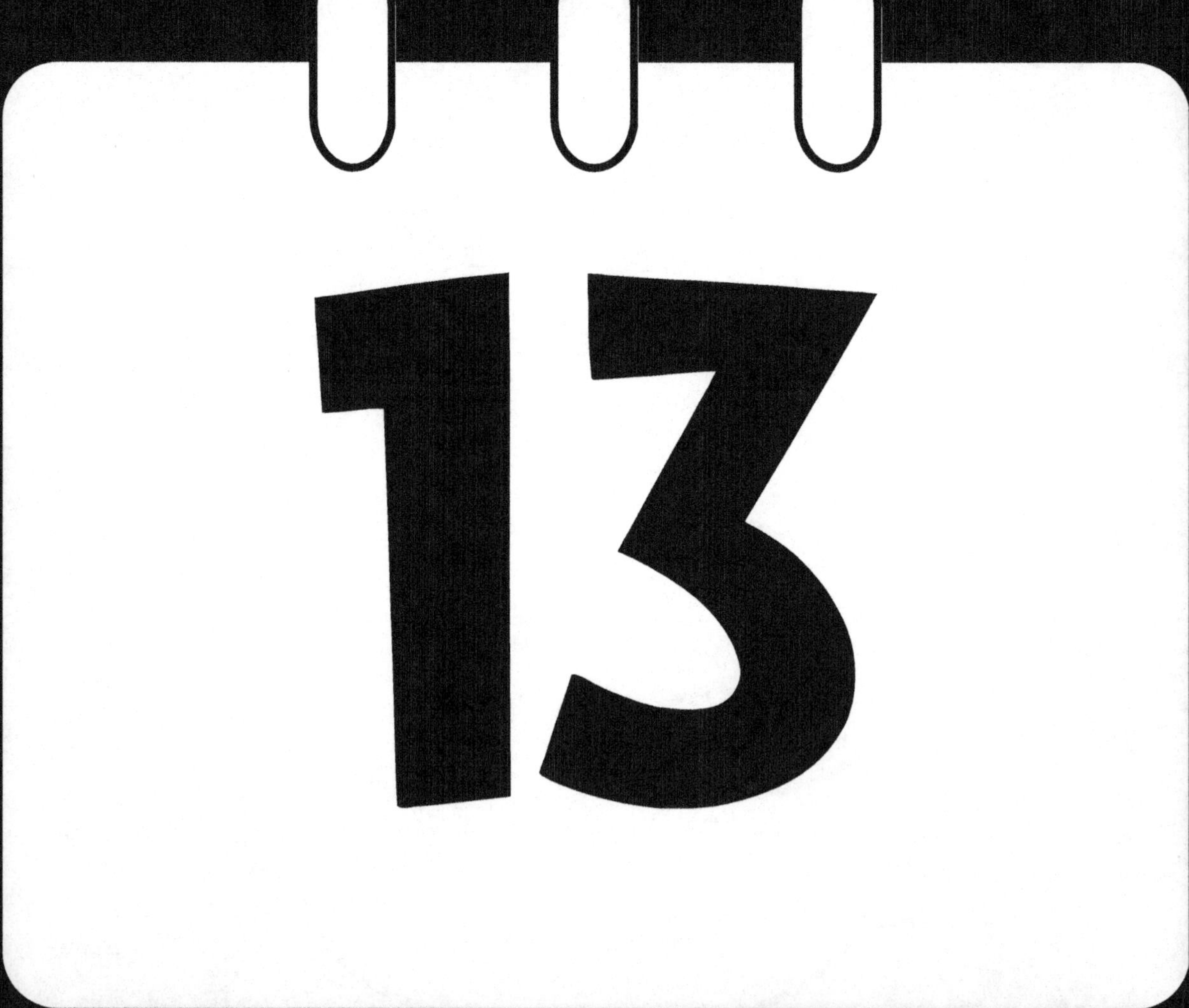
13

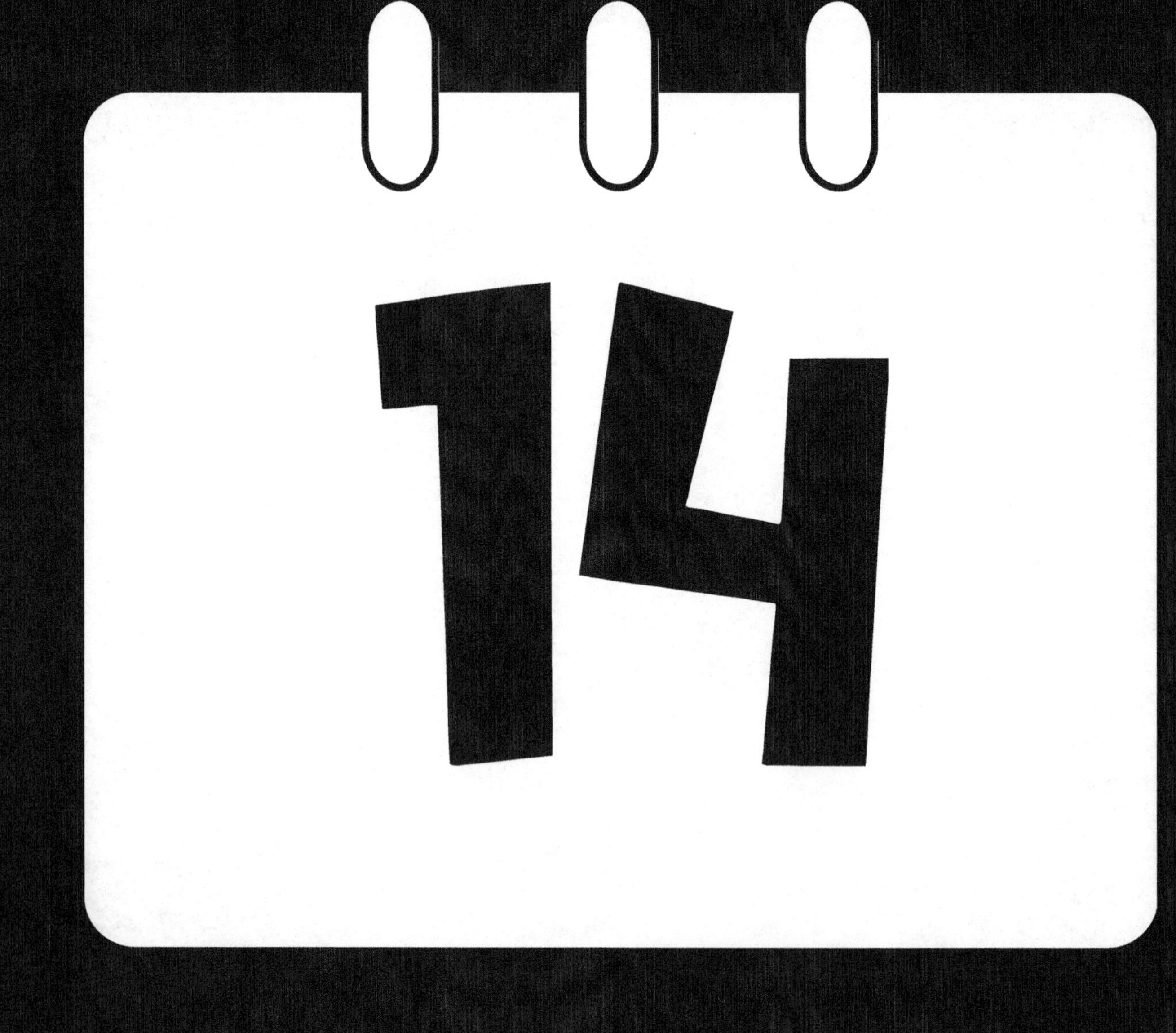
14

LOVE

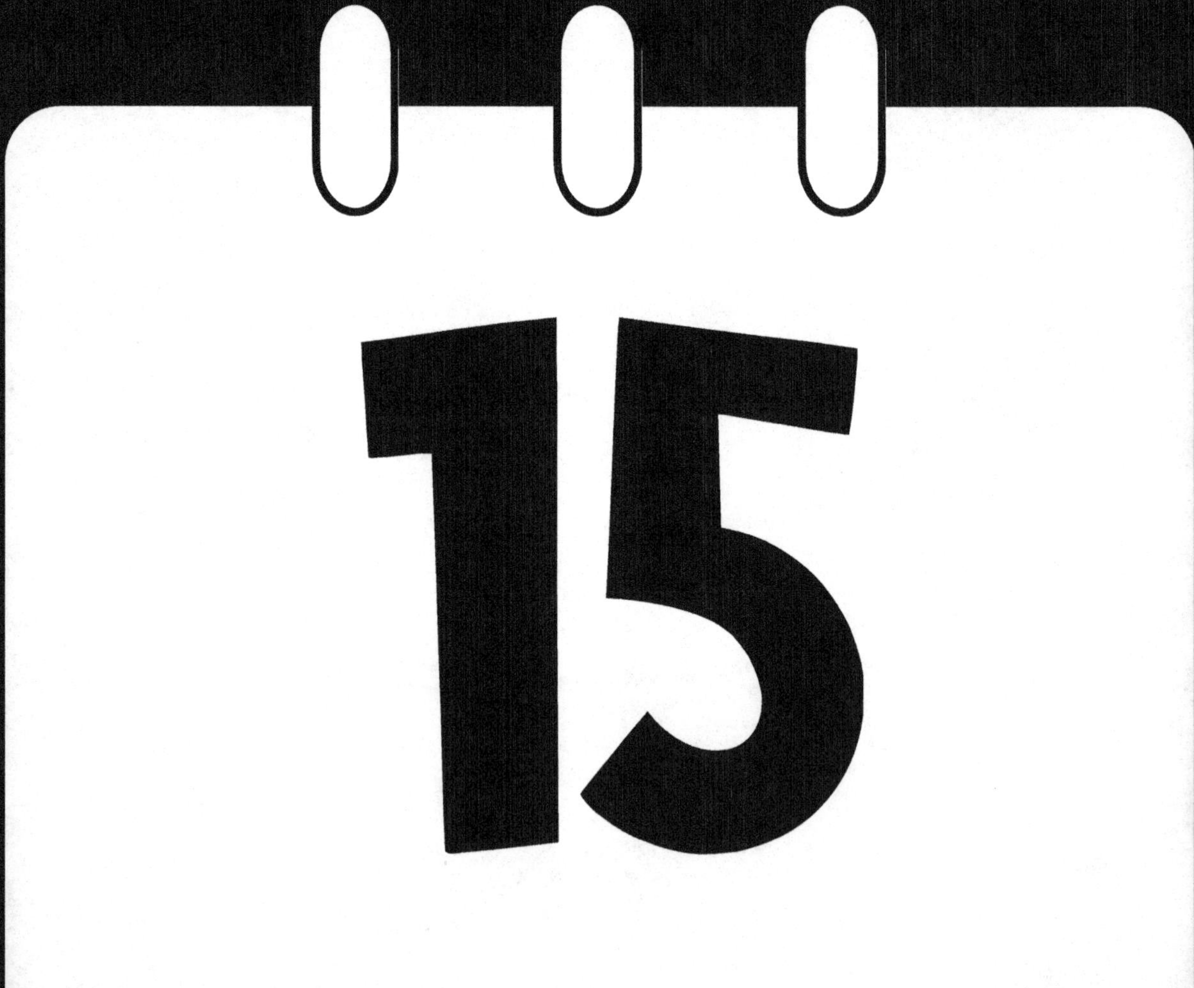
15

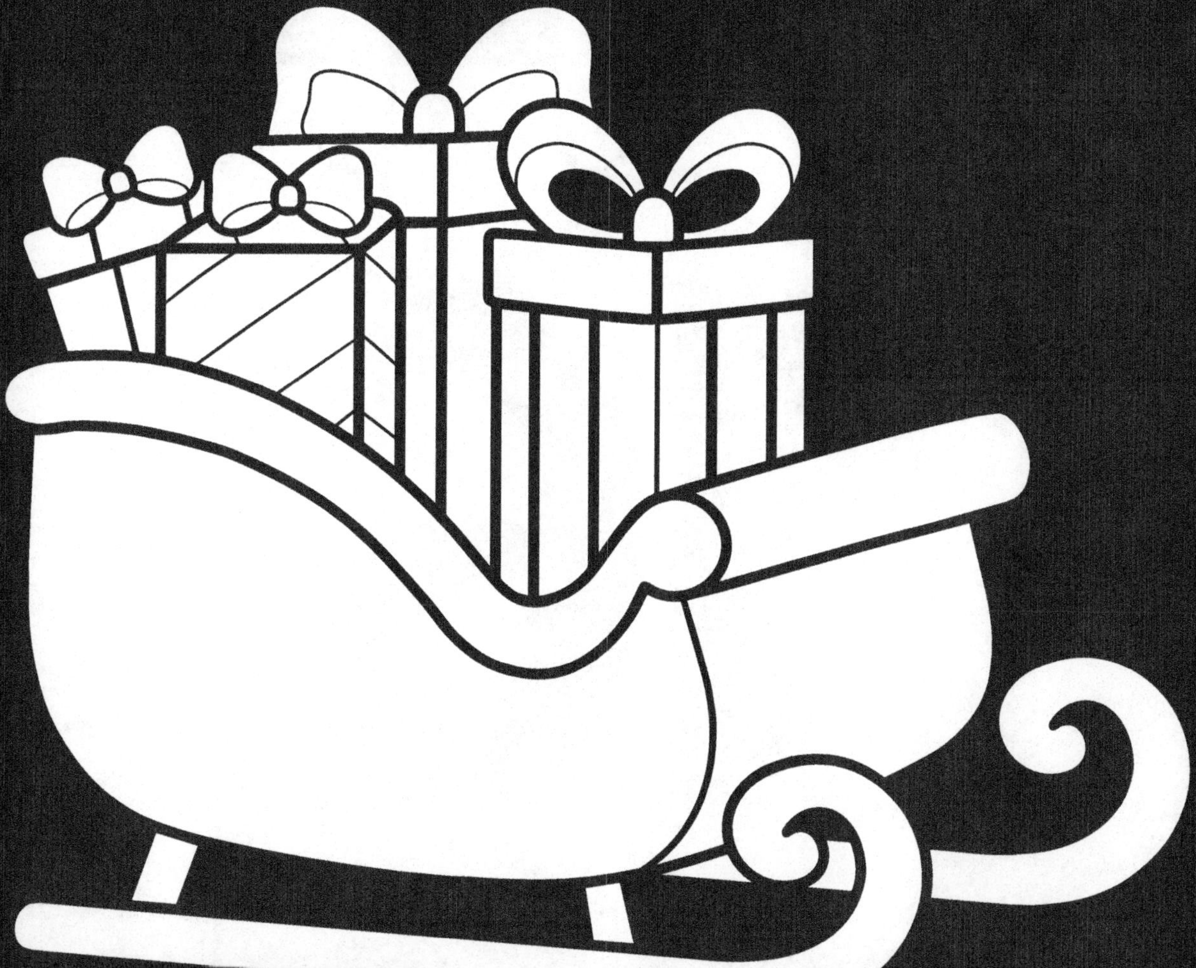

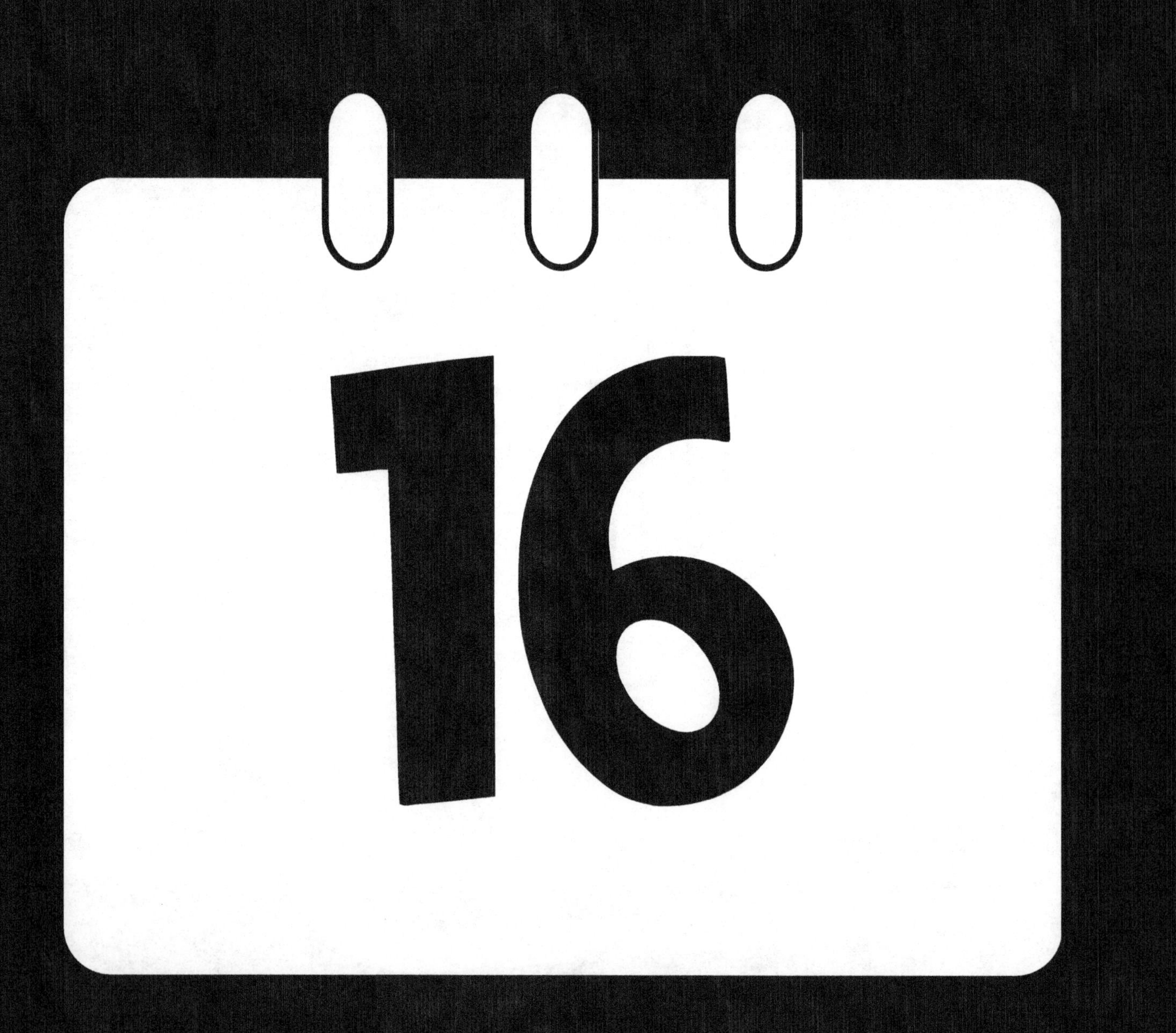
16

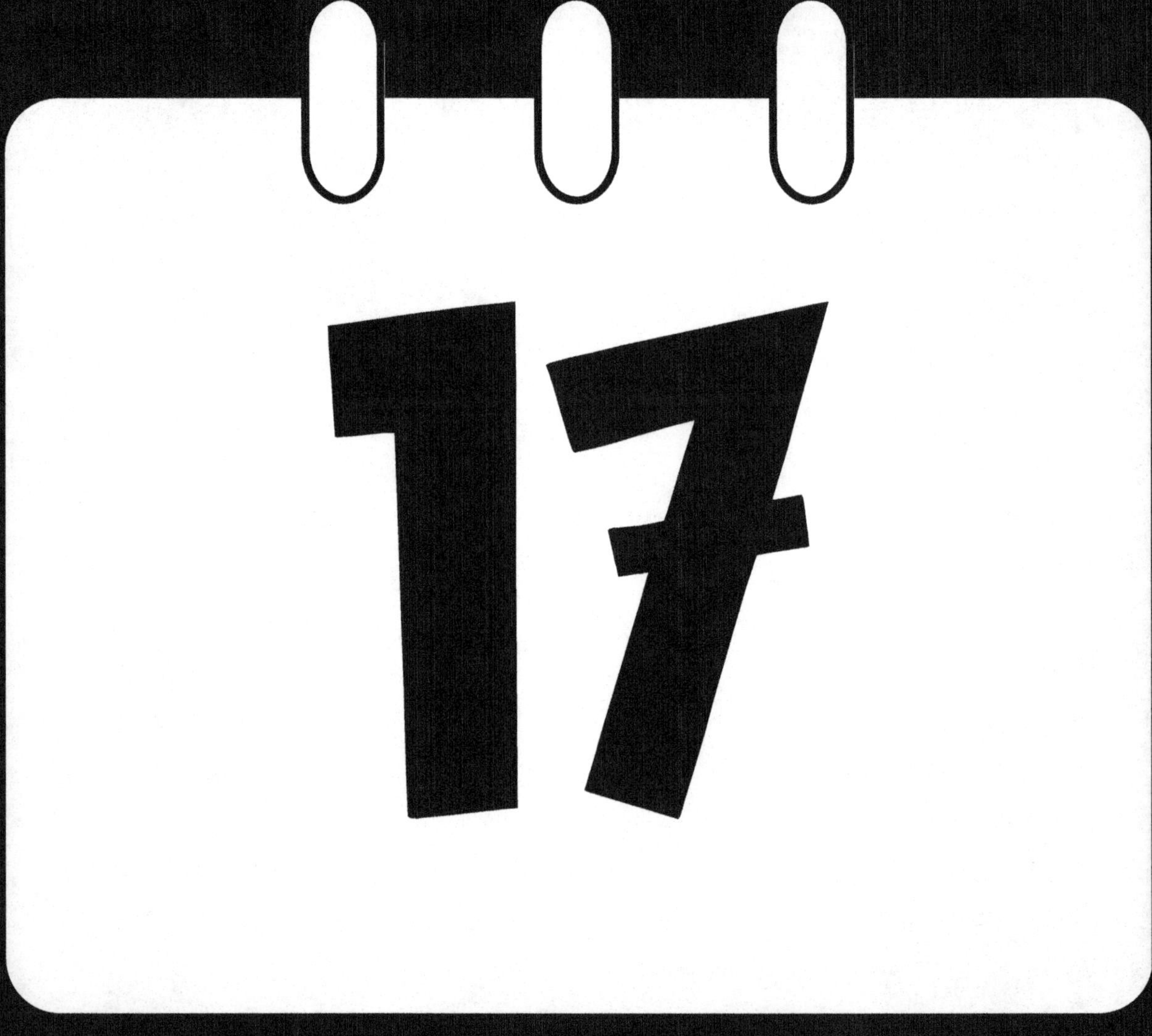
17

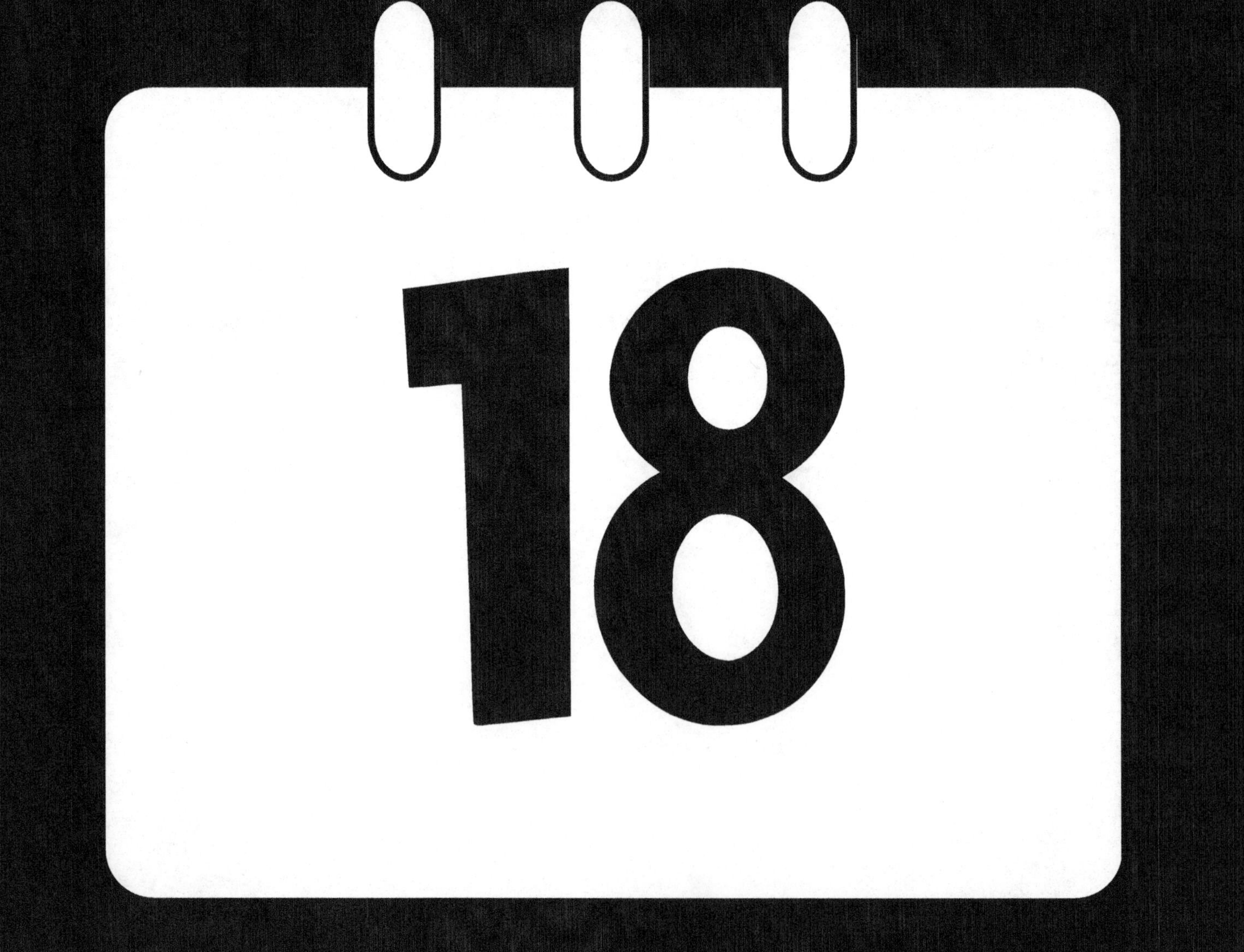
18

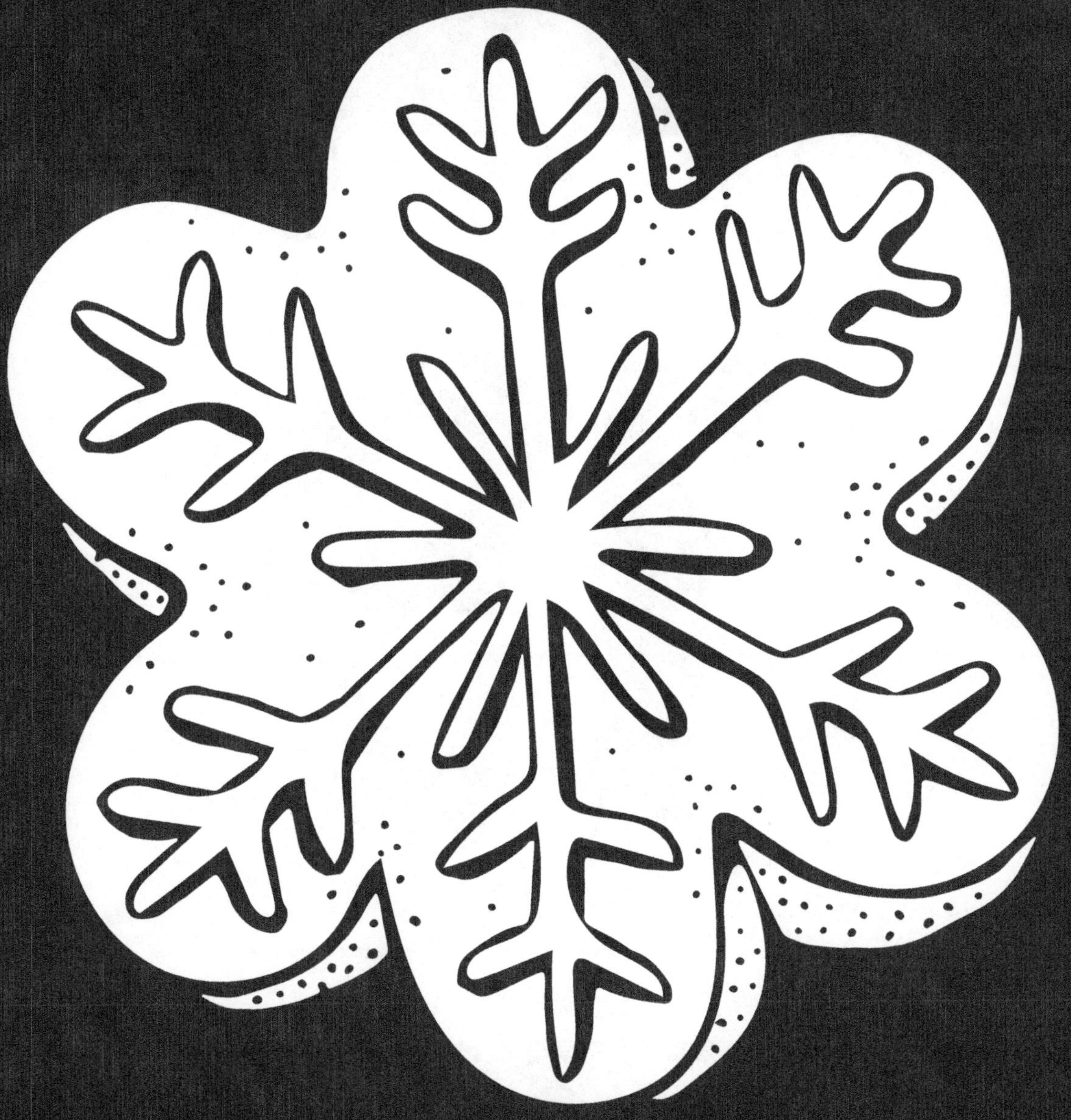

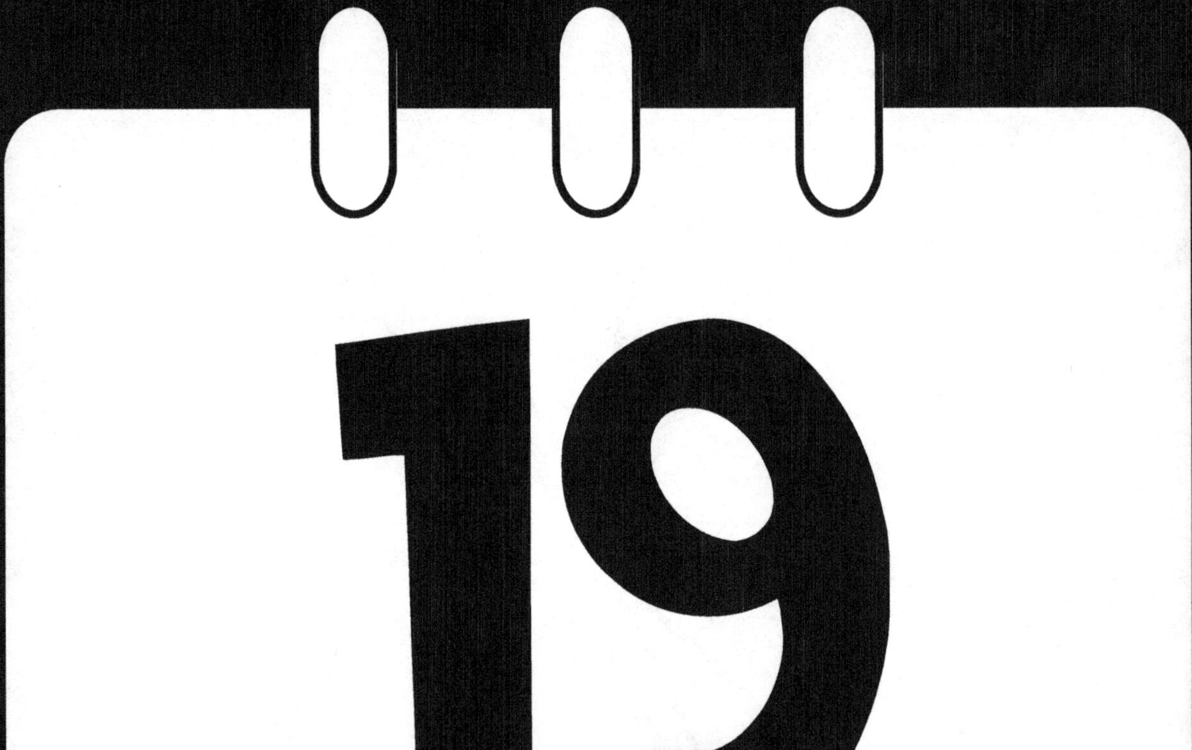
19

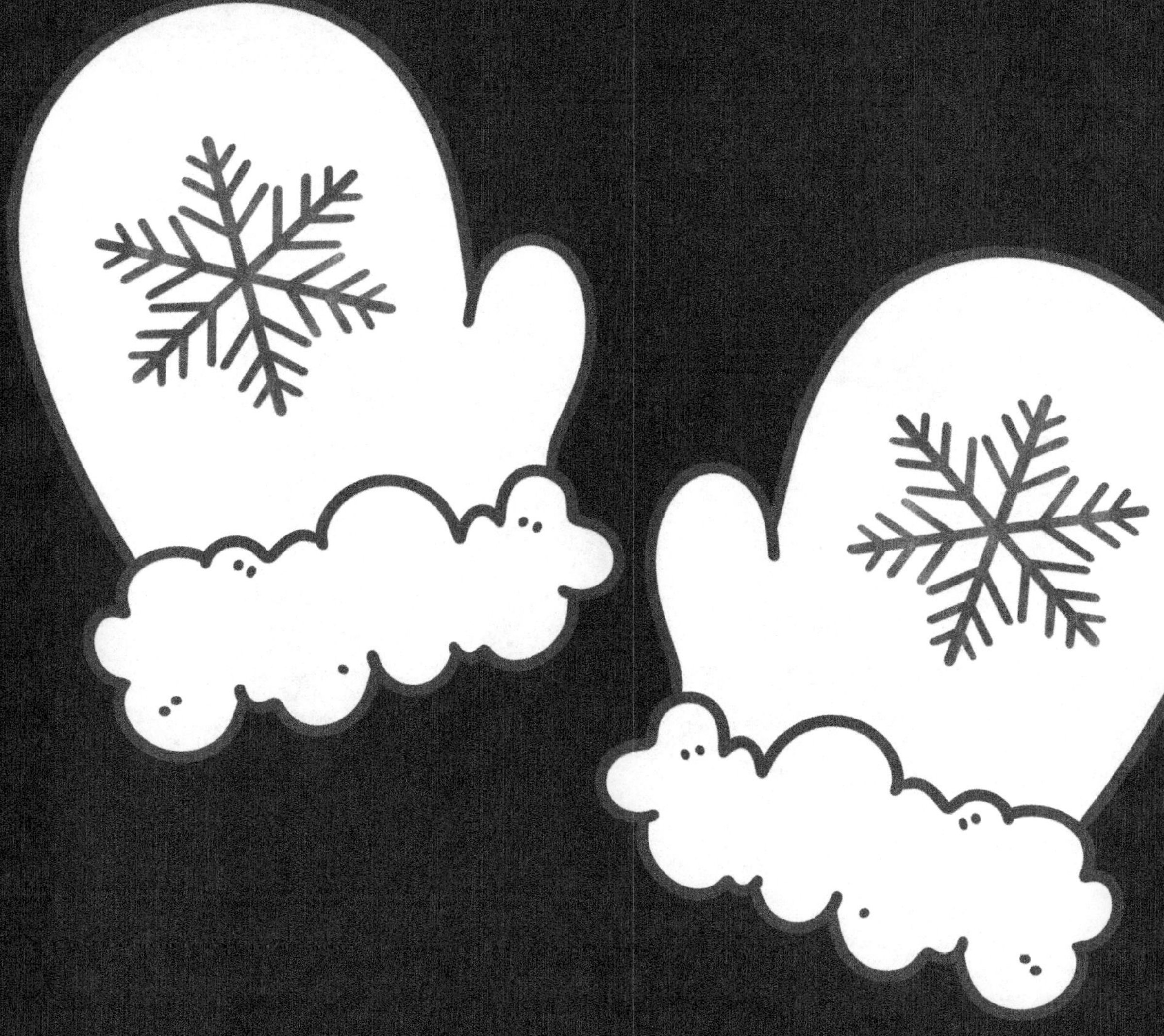

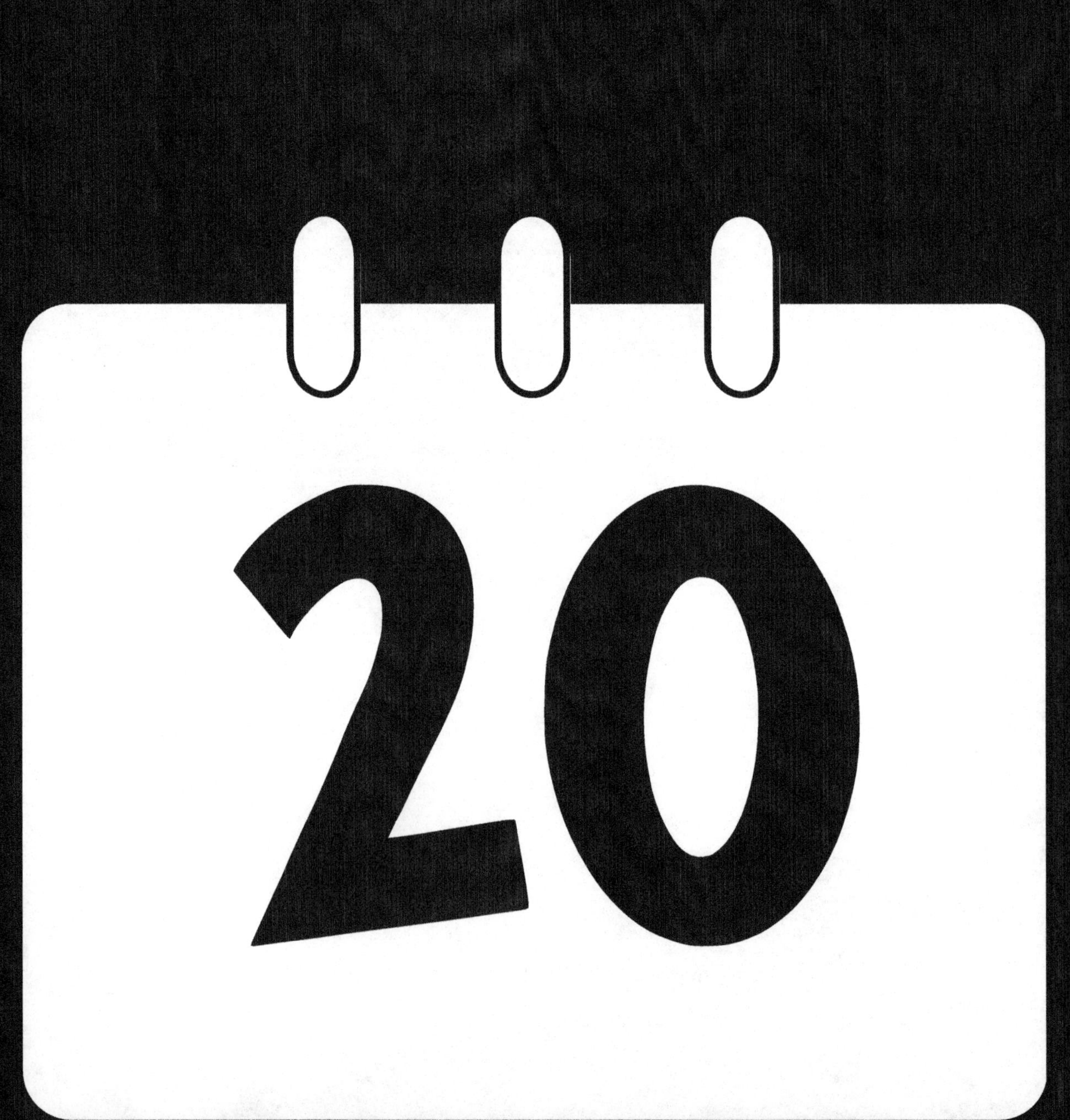
20

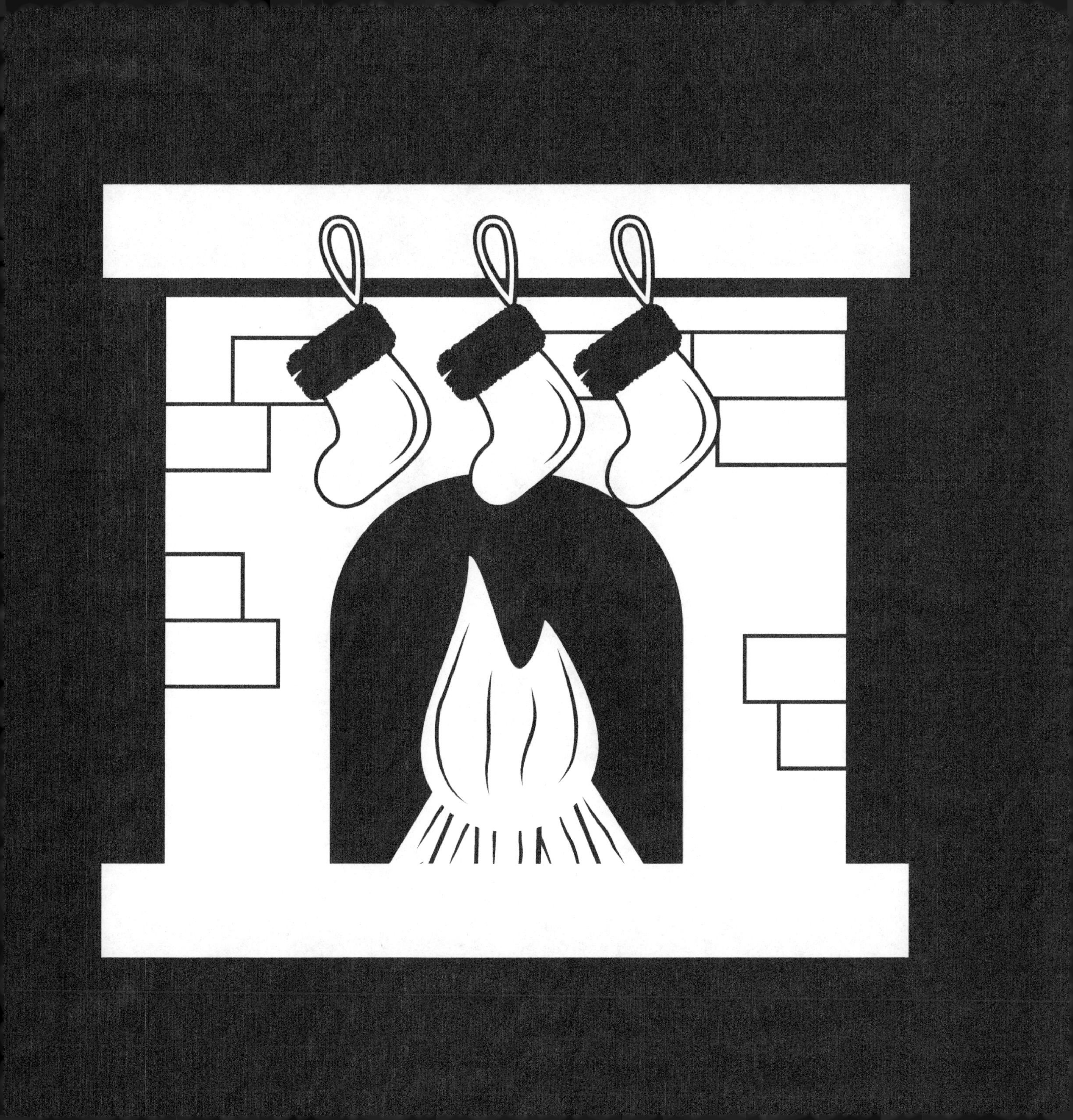

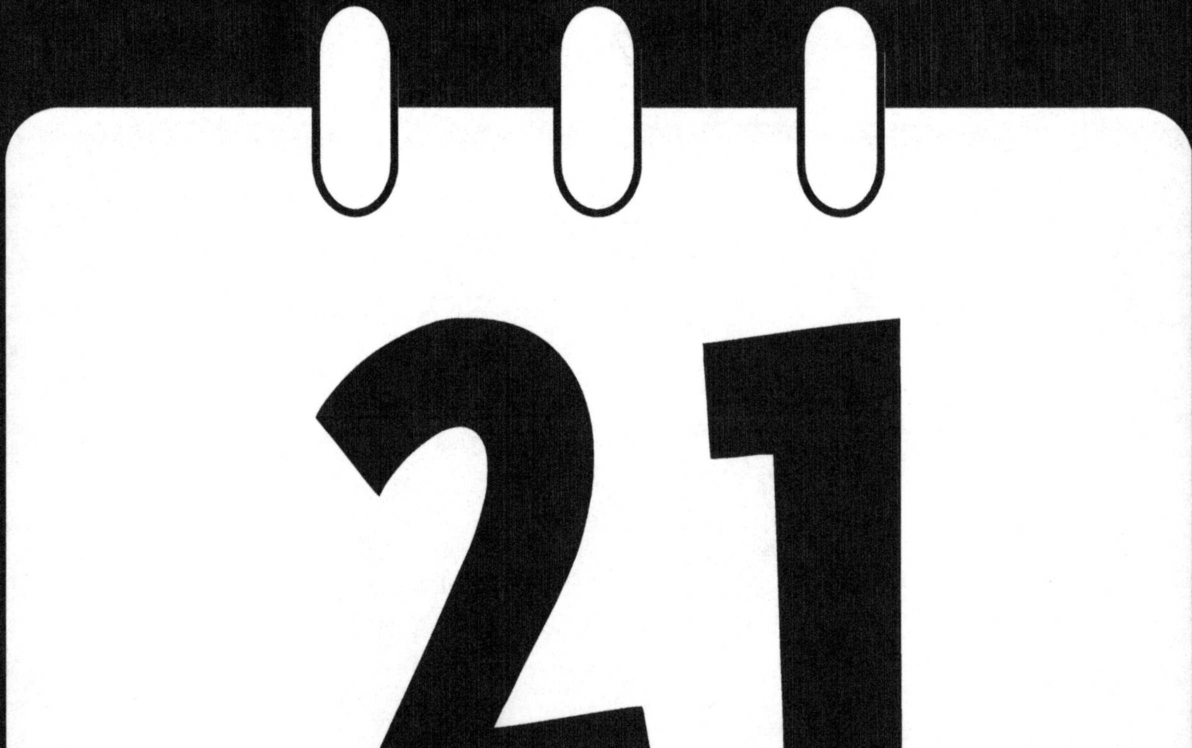
21

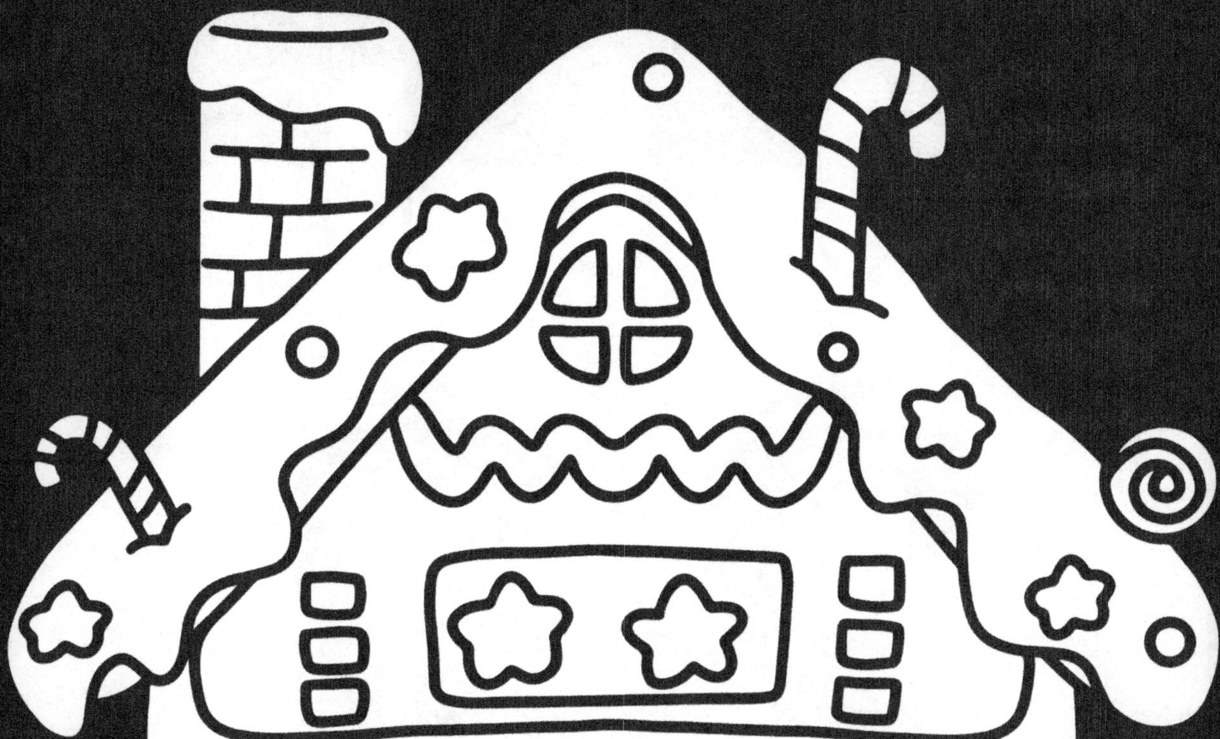

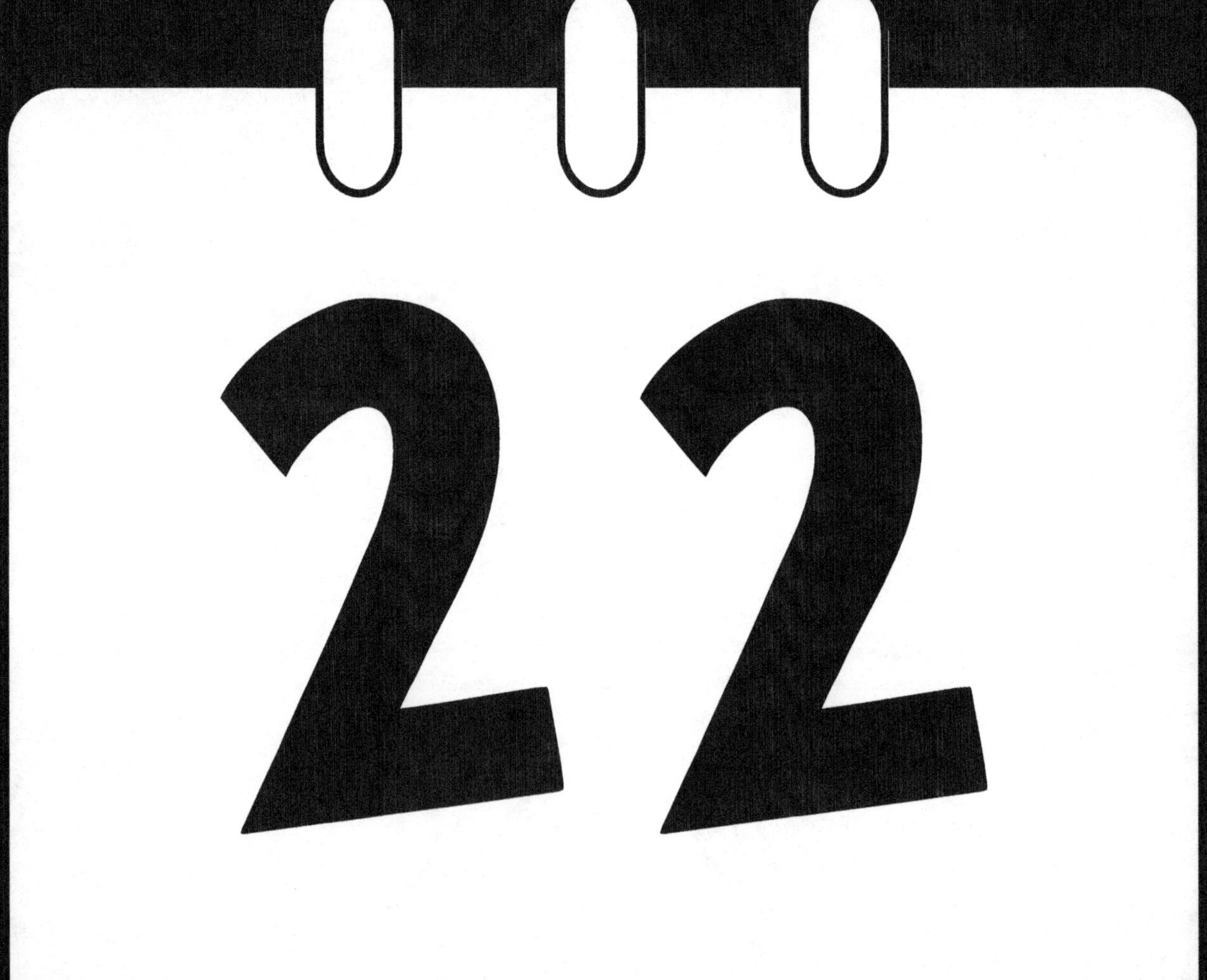
22

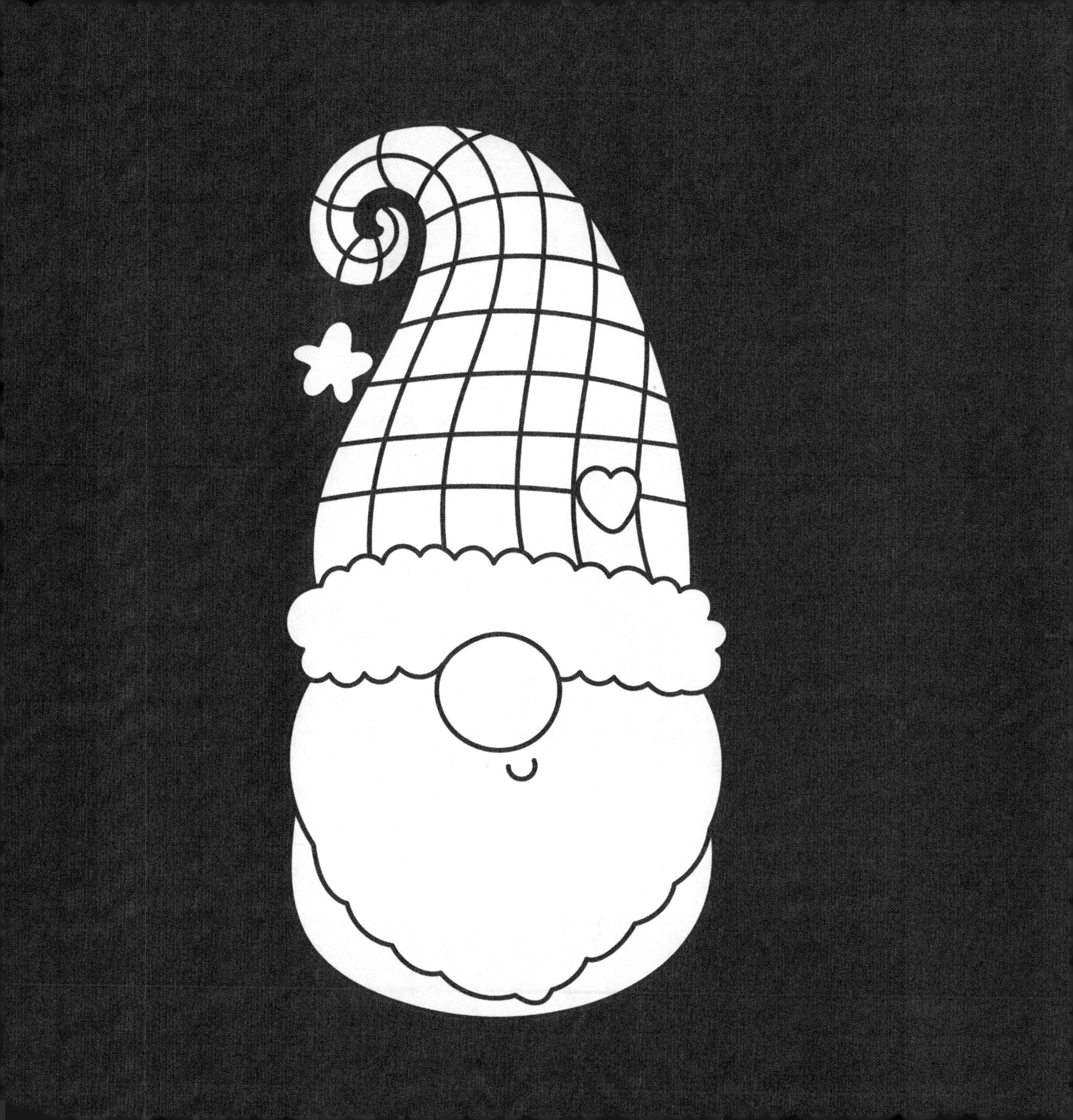

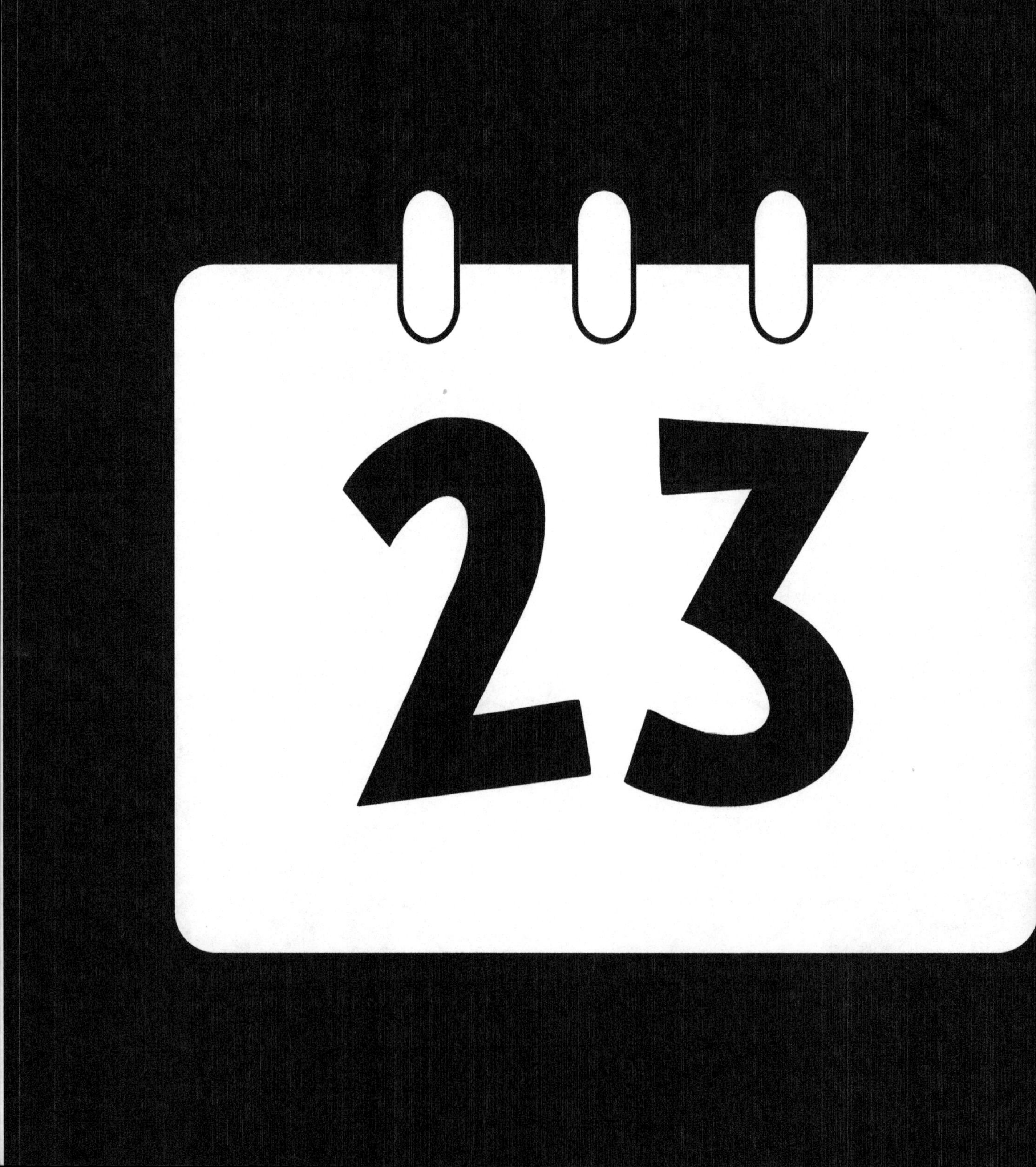
23

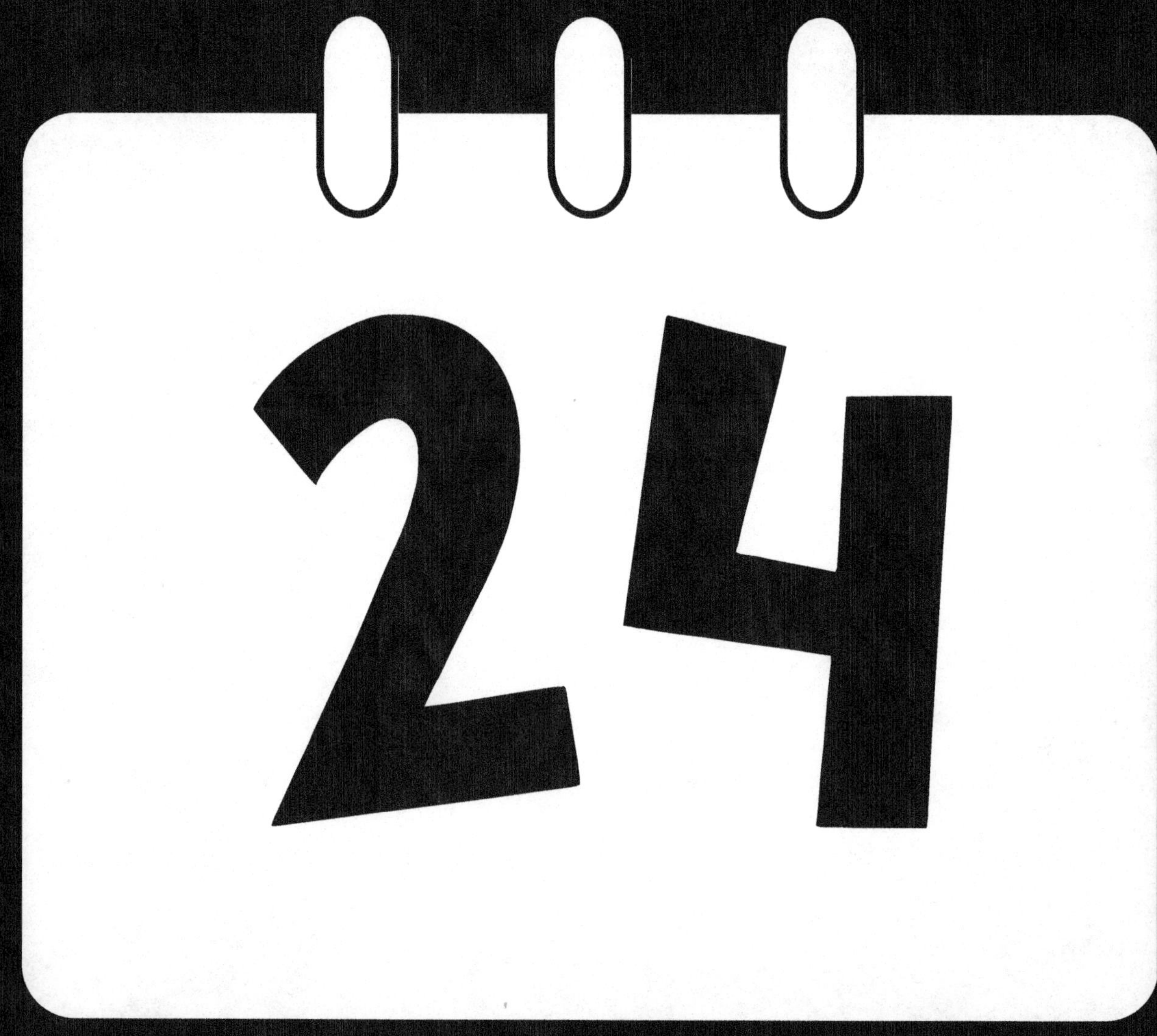
24

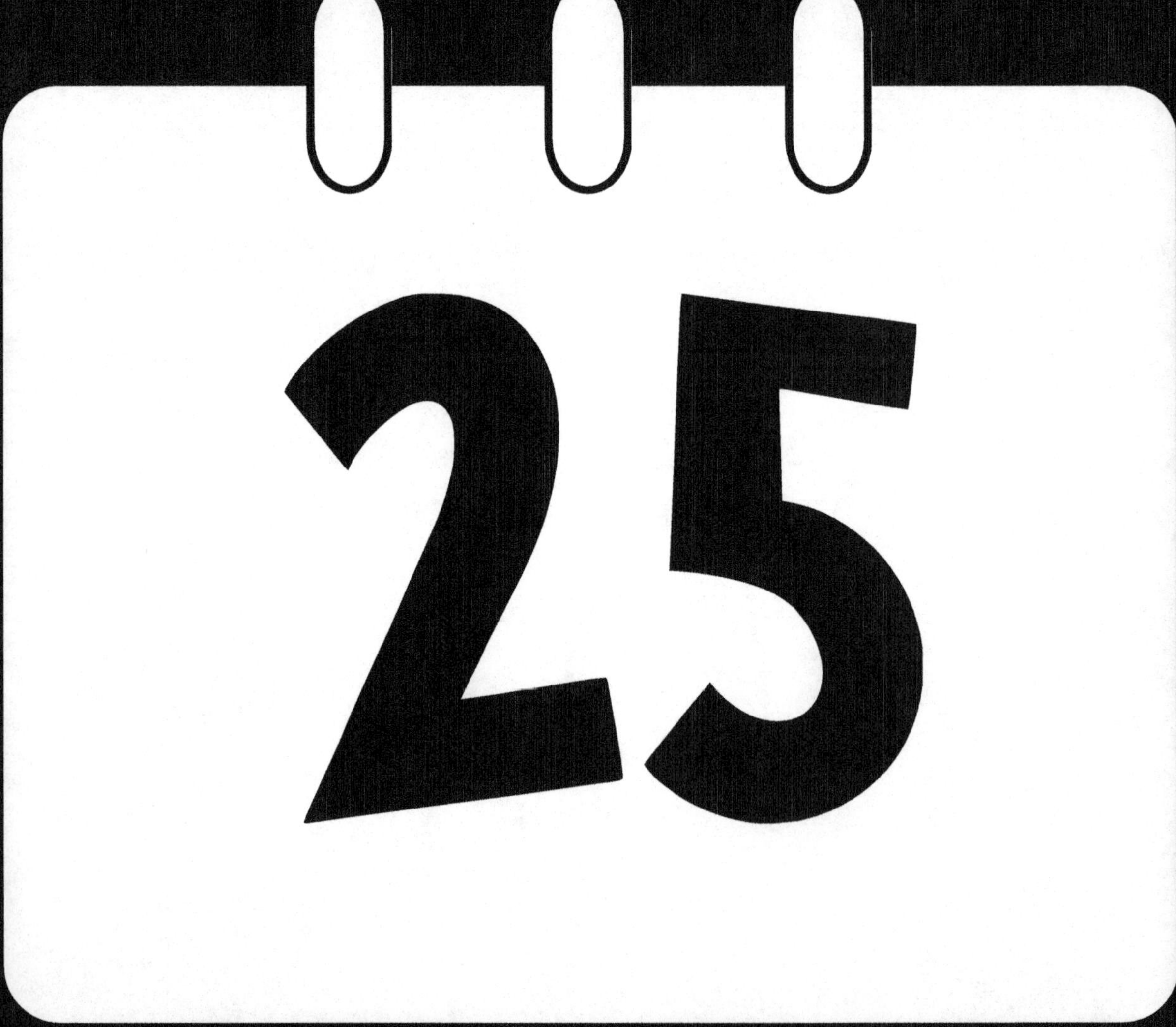
25

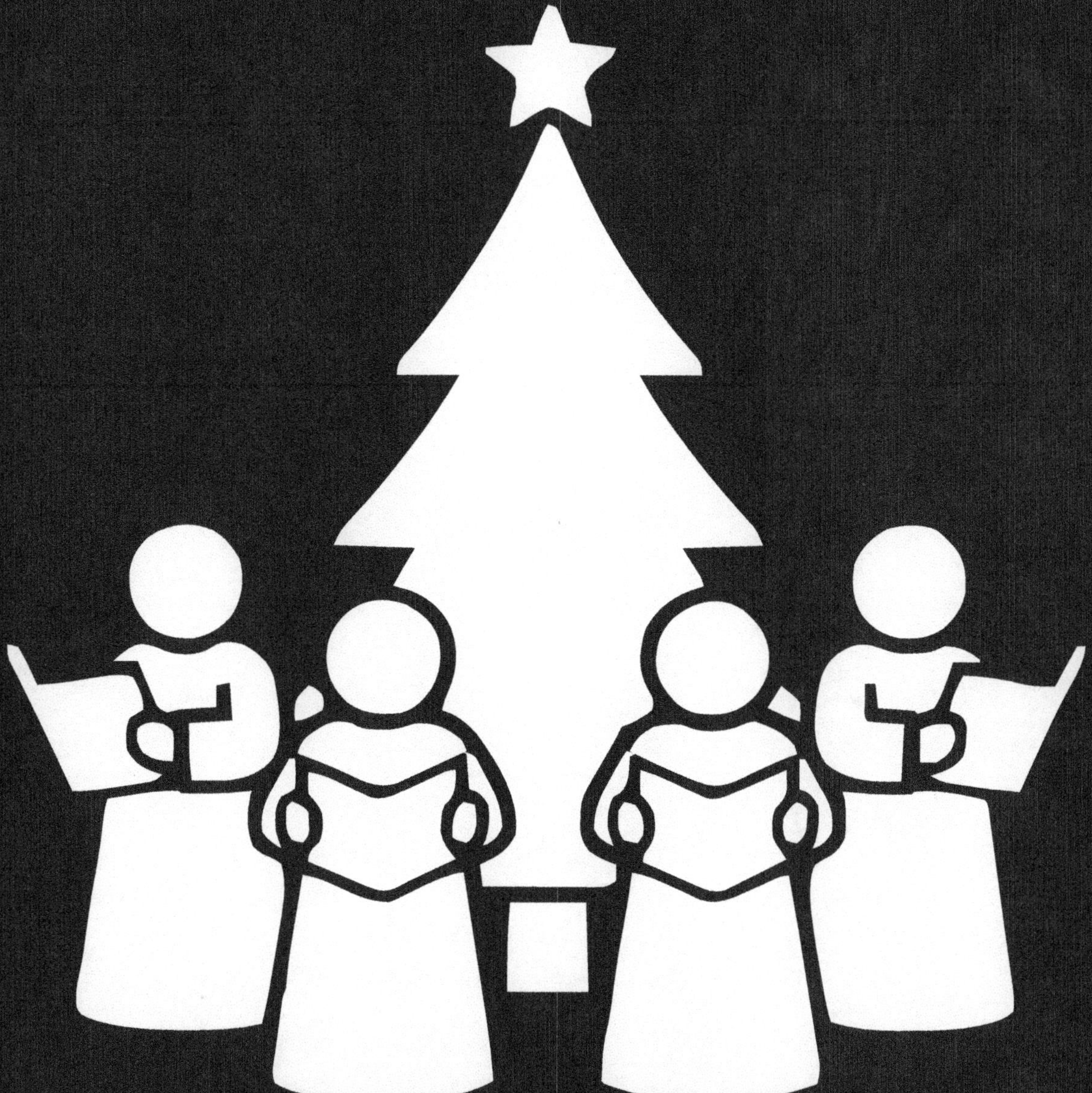

Printed in Dunstable, United Kingdom

72292017R00031